CLASSIC AND
ROMANTIC MUSIC

A Comprehensive Survey

FRIEDRICH BLUME

Translated by M. D. Herter Norton

W · W · NORTON & COMPANY · INC · NEW YORK

FIRST EDITION

Copyright © 1970 by W. W. Norton & Company, Inc. All rights reserved.
Originally published in Germany in "Die Musik in Geschichte und Gegenwart" edited by Friedrich Blume, © by Bärenreiter-Verlag Karl Vötterle
KG 1958, 1963. *Library of Congress Catalog Card No. 78-77390.* Published
simultaneously in Canada by George J. McLeod Limited, Toronto. Printed
in the United States of America.

SBN 393 02137 8 Cloth Edition

SBN 393 09868 0 Paper Edition

1 2 3 4 5 6 7 8 9 0

Contents

*The translator is deeply indebted to Paul Henry Lang
of Columbia University and to David P. Hamilton of W. W.
Norton for substantive and editorial suggestions, as well as to the
author himself for his critical reading. Such assistance carries on
the support lent to our first volume*—Renaissance and Baroque
Music—*by the late Nathan Broder, to whose memory the present
translation is gratefully dedicated.*

M. D. H. N.

Preface

When, in the year 1966, an English version of my two essays on the Renaissance and the Baroque eras in the history of music was being prepared, I tried to explain in a short preface the method I had chosen "to distinguish the two eras from one another, to define their boundaries . . . , and to describe what is characteristic of their music" (p. viii). I need not reiterate what I said there; suffice it to say that my two corresponding articles on the Classic and the Romantic ages in music, here presented in English translation, will follow these same lines. The sum total of these "comprehensive surveys" (as the subtitles of the volumes read) embraces the history of European music from the dusk of the Middle Ages to the dawn of our present time. Whereas, however, Renaissance and Baroque must be regarded as two essentially independent eras of the history of music, marked by definable boundaries with the late Middle Ages on the one side and the Classic-Romantic era on the other, and clearly discernible from one another, the terms Classicism and Romanticism refer to two phenomena not essentially independent, but rather complementing each other and covering one and the same period. It extends roughly from the years when Domenico Scarlatti, Carl Philipp Emanuel Bach, and Jean-Philippe Rameau composed their startling keyboard works, up to the first decades of the 20th century when, with the late works of Richard Strauss, Leoš Janáček, Béla Bartók, Maurice Ravel, and all the rest, the fabric of a time-honored tradition in music gave way to revolutionary currents that had for a long time been washing away the foundations on which that tradition rested.

This is certainly not a very exact definition. But it exactly corresponds to the facts. "Classicism" and "Romanticism" are just two aspects of one and the same musical phenomenon and of one and the same historical period. In terms of chronology, the two labels signify one self-contained age of the history of music; in terms of style, they mark the two facets of this age, the two trends operating within the one fundamental idea of form and expression. There is neither a "Classic" nor a "Romantic" style in music. Both aspects and both trends are continually merging into one. And as there are no discernible styles, there can neither be a clearly definable borderline between Classicism and Romanticism nor a distinct chronology of when the one or the other begins and ends. As I have said in the essay on Romanticism (below, p. 95): "The beginnings of great epochs in music history can be determined, if one takes heed of the arising new and turns away from the still lingering old; but their endings cannot be defined because each epoch lives on under that which follows it." That holds good for Classicism-Romanticism: looking at the palpable new elements in D. Scarlatti, C.P.E. Bach, and Rameau (or, for that matter, in Pergolesi's *La Serva padrona* or in Handel's *Joshua*) leaves no doubt that something new is rising everywhere, the new that is soon to display its two facets—but who dares say when and where and why the age of Classicism and Romanticism died, or even if it really is dead?

The present writer has felt the urgent need and the moral duty not to press the historical facts for answers and therefore has preferred to hint at all the many problems offered by the music of the Classic-Romantic era but to leave open those that do not yet seem answerable. Instead, he feels obligated to say thanks to all those who have assisted in the publication of the English version of these four essays: the understanding translator, Mrs. M. D. Herter Norton; the publishers, W. W. Norton & Company, Inc., the patient advisors and correctors Professor Paul Henry Lang and Mr. David Hamilton. I will never forget the memory of Nathan Broder, to whose unselfish co-operation I largely owe the preparation of the first volume.

Friedrich Blume

CLASSIC AND ROMANTIC MUSIC
A Comprehensive Survey

CLASSIC MUSIC

I

The Concept of the "Classic" as Generally Understood

The words "classic" and "classicism" ("classical" and "classicistic") are frequently applied to music, but for the most part in quite indefinite and often differing senses. They fundamentally imply neither a style period nor a distinct style. On the contrary, the term "classic" embraces phenomena that can recur in the most varied passages and phases of history. In German usage a musical work of art counts as "classic" if it manages to intensify and epitomize in convincing statement and enduring shape the forces of expression and form at work in its own historical context. In this sense, for example, Schubert has often been designated the "classic exponent of the German song," and justly so; the phrase only in appearance contradicts the fact that he is usually ranked historically as a "Romantic": though his general attitude would belong to the Romantic rather than the Classic phase of his historical period, in many of his compositions (*Heidenröslein,* for one) he found the "classic" stamp for the German song for voice and piano. Hence "classic" on the level of a single work, a category of composition, or the like, can very well mean something quite different from "Classic" in the sense of a style period. Schubert drew together the various ways of handling the German song with keyboard accompaniment that had been maturing during the 18th century, bringing them to full fruition; he succeeded in finding for many texts musically satisfying settings which in expressiveness and form have seemed unsurpassable and which have remained lastingly effective.

To be convincing, to be exemplary, and to endure are indispensable ingredients of the "classic." With similar justification, one may say that Palestrina has for centuries been looked upon as the "classic exponent of church music" (and not only Catholic church music). In his strongest compositions he succeeded in linking up the linear-polyphonic style of the *ars perfecta,* so variously typified in the 16th century, with the end-of-the-century's ever-more-disruptive feeling for triadic harmony and, over and above this, in complying, in a manner rarely achieved, with the demands that the music should fit the text and the text be comprehensible. In doing so, Palestrina created convincing works that have been recognized over the centuries as exemplary, not to be excelled in expressiveness and form, and the continuing influence of which still proved inexhaustible in the second quarter of the 19th century, during the movement to restore *a cappella* church music instigated by the so-called Cecilian Societies.

"Classic" as well as "Romantic" authors from Herder to Otto Nicolai and far beyond looked upon Palestrina's music as the very model of "true church music" and saw in him a "classic." His case is, moreover, similar to Schubert's: from the point of view of style history one would place Palestrina at least very close to the Baroque border, if not include him in the Baroque; here, too, the contrast to the "classic" is only apparent, for it has reference to the individual work or the category of composition but not to the style in that particular phase of its historical development. In the term "classic" as applied to Palestrina, there already vibrate overtones of the "classicistic": of the image of battles won, of ripeness achieved, of former contradictions reconciled, all obscurities illumined in an eternal beauty and harmoniousness—a "classicistic" image, in short, similar to that which the later 19th century held of Mozart. Whether the underlying historical idea is "right," that is, whether it can stand up to historical criticism or not, is irrelevant. For use of the word "classic" in this sense implies a standard of values, not a style category and its history. Hence such a use of the term is certainly justified; but one must remain aware that one means something other than a historical style-category.

If, all this notwithstanding, Johann Sebastian Bach is on occasion called the "classic exponent" of Protestant church music, the term includes expression of the fact that in his sacred vocal works or his organ chorales Bach gathered together the various influences and tendencies active in such music before and during his own time, its categories, forms, and styles, blending them with the modern Italian dramatizing trends of his day—basing the whole, however, on the firm ground of the Evangelical liturgy and the Lutheran idea of divine service, and in so doing realized an unsurpassable achievement. The fact that his works indeed received only qualified recognition as "exemplary" and were at first displaced by others differentiates his case from Schubert's and Palestrina's. But then, in the Romantic era, the influence of Bach's music matured immeasurably—that is, proved its durability—and in so doing confirms the idea of what is "classic."

In this general sense one may regard Marenzio, say, as the classic exponent of the Italian madrigal, Josquin as the classic exponent of the Netherlandish Mass. Ambros believed that in the latter he could explicitly vouch for its "golden purity," "drosslessness," and "purest beauty." With his perception that Josquin's music operated as much through keeping the mind occupied as through the "afflation" of some inexplicable "magic," that its part-writing was at once "full of life" and "discreet," that it embodied a "clarified, pure style-ideal," Ambros was expressing his own intuitively classicistic view without, however, applying the concept of "classic" directly to Josquin.

While one cannot deny that such a use of the word may be justified, it is certain that so generally adopted an application of the concept finally renders it empty. The word easily goes flat when used in this way and comes to mean not much more than the "high point" of a category or field of expression. What has preceded the high point then recedes into the light of something preliminary, questing, and tentative, and, seen from this view, what follows the high point necessarily appears as "baroque" exaggeration or "classicistic" leveling.[1] From here on it is but a step to the cult of the

1. Thus maintains Charles Lalo in his *Esquisses d'une esthétique musicale scientifique*, Paris, 1908. (Second edition published in 1939 as *Éléments d'une esthétique musicale scientifique*.)

hero: music history appears not as an infinitely multiple interweaving of living forces that continually overlap, displace, complement, and kindle each other, not as a chain of forms of expression mutually conditioning each other, but as a series of ascents, high points, and declines at each temporary apex of which one or more masters stand, compared with whom all others are but forerunners or epigones. In history thus pictured, Beethoven all too easily appears as a "classic," not because he welded together in the power of his personality the forces flowing to him from the 18th century, and shaped them into convincing forms of enduring value, but because he "stood upon the shoulders of Haydn and Mozart," because he perfected what others before him had only striven toward, so that the masters of the Romantic era appear as mannerizing exaggerators or epigonous followers.

It is obvious that such a picture is based on irresponsible simplifications and does justice neither to the hero nor to the composers surrounding him. That Beethoven is, in a certain sense, a high point no one will dispute, but that he is also entirely different from the composers about him, that his predecessors as well as his followers are personalities in their own right, is suppressed in the process; the concept of the "classic" is rendered hollow. In every unfolding period of history there are present from the start both those forces that lead to such a high point and those that press toward "baroque" exaggeration or "classicistic" leveling. When a chosen spirit is able to unite in himself the progressive, retardative, and manifoldly criss-crossing tendencies of his time and put them to convincing and lasting effect, the result is an achievement of highly personal character, which however cannot in every case lay claim to counting as "classic." This is the error into which, for example, Adelmo Damerini falls [2] when he extols Bach's *St. Matthew Passion* and Verdi's *Falstaff* in one and the same breath as models of the highest classicism.

In its general application, the word "classic" does retain a useful meaning, mostly when it refers to a particular type of composition (as in the aforementioned examples of Schubert and Pales-

2. Adelmo Damerini, *Classicismo e romanticismo,* Florence, 1942.

trina). In this sense Beethoven may be called a "classic" master of
the symphony, the piano sonata, the string quartet, without
implying any judgment about his position in the history of styles.
The distinction between the "classic" as a convincing and enduring
solution to the problem of creative shaping in a work of art or a
category of composition on the one hand, and on the other as a
concept in the history of style, makes the constant quarrel, which
flares up even today—was Beethoven a "Classic" or a "Romantic"?—appear quite futile: he was both, depending on the meaning
one attributes to the words.

As a concept in the history of style, the word "classic" takes
on a precise and comprehensive meaning only when placed in a
context, not of rise or decline, not of classicism or baroque, not of
precursorship or successorship, but of something essentially conge-
neric—in other words: when in a given period the *one* fundamental idea of creative form splits into two lines, interpenetrating and
reciprocally influential, yet at the same time striving away from
and contradicting each other. This is what happens in the period
that in the more specific music-historical sense is now called the
Classic-Romantic.

II

"Classic" and "Romantic"

In 19th-century music historiography, the word "Classic" came to refer to a style period the beginning of which may be set for Germany at about the generation of Quantz and Hasse, at latest with the sons of Bach and their contemporaries, and for Italy with Domenico Scarlatti and his successors. The end of that period, however, cannot be strictly defined, because the "Classic era" in its unity and its conflict with the "Romantic era" extended through the whole 19th century and far into the 20th, even experiencing an apparent after-bloom in the "neo-Classicism" of around 1930. When and where the word "Classic" entered into the vocabulary of music history cannot be exactly determined. In any case, it first received the meaning imputed to it today through the antagonism between more "classically" and more "romantically" inclined musicians and writers (the significance of each word always being decidedly relative here). Only from Romantic music's "taking the upper hand" and from the opposition it met (to which many important musicians of the 19th century belonged) did the need arise to find a name for that which would serve as an esthetic norm and a bulwark against what was felt to be a continuously intensified overexcitement of musical means and an exaggerated individualization; only then did it become customary to speak of a "classic" beauty in contrast to what were considered "excrescences." Whereas for literature Schiller was already using the expression "classic" and Goethe applied it as a contrast to "romanticism," in music the word "romantic" was apparently used earlier than "classic." Significantly, even Heinrich Christoph Koch's

Handwörterbuch of 1807, for example, contains a short article entitled "Romantisch," while an entry for "Klassisch" is still missing; yet in his *Lexikon* of 1802 one seeks even the entry "Romantisch" in vain. Around that time this latter word seems to have become a musical term in German. According to Damerini [3] it was first employed in music in Grétry's *Mémoires ou Essais* (1789), and Condorcet used it in *La Chronique de Paris* (April 1, 1793) to characterize the music of Méhul.

If the many attempts to define the nature of "the classic" in imaginative literature are subject to countless misunderstandings and obscurities, this is to an even greater extent the case in music. There are only approximate definitions, and probably only such are possible, because every definition must consider the "classic" in its relation to the "romantic," since both these style concepts are basically one, being but two different refractions of the one concept of shaping. There is no "Classic" style period in the history of music, only a "Classic-Romantic" one, within which those forms that are "classically" determined can at most be characterized as phases. "Classic style means the perfect blending into esthetic form of the individually contradictory. The concept of perfection that comes to expression in this process results from complete self-reliance, total self-dependence of the creative spirit. Without this inner independence and self-generated sense of responsibility of the creative artist, a classic art is inconceivable." [4]

In classicism the antinomies of individuality and historical currents are neutralized through the power of a creative personality in the convincing (and, one may add, unique) form of the work of art. In the classic sense, the work of art is a whole and partakes of all humanity; the more the idea of humanity shines through it, the higher it stands. "Every individual human being," says Schiller, "is less a human being by just so much as he is an individual; every way of feeling is just so much less essentially and purely human as it is peculiar to one particular object. Only in the casting away of the haphazard and in pure expression of the essential does the

3. *Ibid.,* p. 11.
4. Rudolf Gerber, in *Die Sammlung,* IV/11 (November 1949), 656.

great style lie" [5] (which here as good as implies "classic style").
The antinomy of necessity and freedom is surmounted and conquered in the classic work of art through the analogy between
inner feeling and outward form. Out of feeling, form takes shape
ever anew as its ideal expression. "But now the whole effect of
music . . . consists in accompanying and rendering perceptible the
inmost movements of the soul through analogous external movements. Now since those inmost movements (human by nature) act
through strict laws of necessity, this necessity and distinctness also
pass over into the external movements through which they are expressed; and in this way it becomes comprehensible how by means
of that symbolic act the common natural phenomena of sound
. . . can participate in the esthetic worth of human nature." [6] And
again "In the beautiful stability of a musical composition is re-
flected the still more stable beauty of a morally attuned soul." [7] A
decisive element in this concept of the classic work of art is that
the composer creates the form only and thus attunes "the disposition to a certain way of feeling and to assimilation of certain
ideas" but leaves the finding of some content in this form to "the
listener's power of imagination." Thus from the "classic" is ex-
cluded every sort of music that undertakes to lead the listener's
feeling in too definite, too individual a manner, to give his fantasy
and collaboration too definite a direction, and to infringe upon his
autonomy as co-creator. And at the same time every music is ex-
cluded that either serves externally set purposes or aims at giving
direct expression to certain contents through imitation and picto-
rialization. The imitation of Nature or of the affects, which in the
esthetic of the Baroque and still in that of the age of the Enlightenment was held to be the principal subject matter of music, is now
totally rejected. Hugo Goldschmidt [8] and Walter Serauky [9] have
shown in detail how the concept of imitation as the main subject

5. *Über Matthissons Gedichte.*
6. *Ibid.*
7. *Ibid.*
8. Hugo Goldschmidt, *Die Musikästhetik des 18. Jahrhunderts,* Zurich
and Leipzig, 1915.
9. Walter Serauky, *Die musikalische Nachahmungsästhetik im Zeit-
raum von 1700 bis 1850,* Münster, 1929.

of music in the period from Charles Batteux, say, to Herder was
increasingly replaced by the slowly developing idealistic concept of
music. Johann Adam Hiller in the foreword to his translation of
Michel Paul de Chabanon's *Observations,* which he published in
1781 under the title *Über die Musik und deren Wirkungen,* "con-
clusively rejected the doctrine of imitation." [10] The composer
should create autonomously out of his own experience, but the listener, too, must autonomously collaborate at fulfillment. Musical
form should sublimate, in symbols, what moved the artist and what
he wanted to express; to interpret the symbol is the private and in-
alienable right of the listener. This is reason enough why every attempt to underlay Classic music with certain definite and obligatory content (as Arnold Schering, for example, undertook to do
for Beethoven) springs from the Romantic and not from the Classic point of view. The Romanticists were the first to impute to
music concrete content, condemning the listener to passivity. Equilibrium in the functions of artist and listener is precisely the characteristic of the Classic point of view.

In the case of vocal music such an equilibrium is also demanded in the relationship between composer and poet. Here, too,
the point is that the composer has only to create a symbolic form
exactly fitting the poetic substratum but may neither subordinate
himself to the poem nor do violence to it through all too definite
an interpretation. In this sense Goethe demands a "symbolism for
the ear." He wrote to Zelter (March 6, 1810): "Only one thing I
want to mention, that you have made use in a very significant
way of that for which I have no name but which is called imitation, painting and I know not what else, and which in others becomes very faulty and degenerates unduly. It is a symbolism for
the ear, through which the subject, to the extent that it is in motion or not in motion, is neither imitated nor painted but is
brought forth in the imagination in a quite particular and incomprehensible way, that which is expressed seeming to bear almost
no relationship to that which expresses it." And again, ten years

10. According to Anna Amalie Abert, in *Die Musik in Geschichte und
Gegenwart* (hereinafter referred to as MGG), article *Hiller.*

later (May 2, 1820): "The purest and highest painting in music is that which you yourself also practice; the point is to put the listener in the mood indicated by the poem; the power of his imagination thereupon shapes the configurations to which the text gives rise without itself knowing how it arrives at doing this." Schiller's "casting away of the haphazard" and "beautiful expression of the essential," the renunciation of the too-individual, coincide with Goethe's censure of imitation and painting; both recognize that the composer, through the "symbolic" act with which he creates in his form an "analogy" to human feelings, calls forth emotions and ideas in an "incomprehensible way"; the preludes in Haydn's *Creation* are at one point expressly referred to as an example.

If the life of the soul is given musical form in such manner, this depends not upon reproduction of some individual item but only upon this world of feeling being grasped in its entirety and shaped into an all-inclusive form. "What springs from the most deeply felt unity of music with words or with a character to be presented . . . , music that forms an 'inclusive' whole only with something else . . . , is music according to the view of Zelter and Goethe," says Paul Mies.[11] And Goethe writes to Karl Wilhelm von Humboldt (March 14, 1803): "He [Zelter] admirably catches the character of such a whole, recurring in identical strophes, so that it is felt again in every single part; whereas others, by a so-called through-composition, destroy the impression of the whole with obtrusive details." Goethe's diaries and yearbooks of 1801 also speak of the "reprehensibility" of through-composing, by which the "over-all" character is annulled and "a false participation in detail is demanded."

It is in this way that what Schiller calls the "grand style" comes into being. The word "classic" is not yet applied to music; only gradually, in connection with the literary quarrel over "Classicism" and "Romanticism," did it pass into music also. Consequently, no distinction is yet made here between "classic" and "romantic" in music. Music, pursued from points of view such as Goethe's, embodies human emotions and imaginings, idealizes

11. In *Zeitschrift für Musikwissenschaft*, XIII (1930–31), 437.

them, and enhances them to universal validity. It takes in the whole man and must, therefore, in itself create a perfect whole. Thus will a musical work of art come into being that is in some "incomprehensible way" consummately true, convincing, and universally valid, though its content cannot be translated into words and to that extent remains mysterious.

It was Herder who wrote: "Music rouses a series of intimate feelings, true but not clear, not even perceptual, only most obscure. You, young man, were in its dark auditorium; it lamented, sighed, stormed, exulted; you felt all that, you vibrated with every string. But about what did it—and you with it—lament, sigh, exult, storm? Not a shadow of anything perceptible. Everything stirred only in the darkest abyss of your soul, like a living wind that agitates the depths of the ocean." [12] Upon this follows the definite renunciation of rationalism and of the Encyclopedists, who had required of music "imitation" and "the realistic rendering of feelings": the world of music is a fictitious world, valid not in that it translates into tones what can be perceived, contemplated, felt, but in that it sublimates what has been perceived, contemplated, felt, into a language of truth entirely private, mysterious, but deeply moving and understandable to all—that very language of symbols "for the ear." Herder, too, expressly demands of music truthfulness and wholeness. Wholeness, to quote Wiora, means "that no layer of human nature is omitted or stunted: it should contain not only what is subconscious and perceptible by the senses, but also the vibrant motor energy of the body, as well as the warm sentiments of the heart and the wise manifestations of the spirit." [13] Truthfulness means that the symbolic forms should be cast ever anew not from the current coin of inherited formulas but from the genuine gold of experience.

In order to produce in this fully sovereign manner, the composer needs to be set free of tasks and purposes imposed upon his creativity from outside. Perhaps one of the most decisive steps

12. Johann G. Herder, *Sämtliche Werke,* ed. by B. Suphan, IV, Berlin, 1877–1913, p. 161 f.
13. Walter Wiora, *Herders Ideen zur Geschichte der Musik,* in *Im Geiste Herders,* Kitzingen, 1953, p. 79.

away from all older views on music toward the Classic was taken
in the freeing of composition from all obligation to imitate, to express, to represent, to serve, even to entertain, so that now music
stood altogether on its own. For the first time in history there
arises the idea that music, like all art indeed, has no "purpose," but
exists for its own sake. In opposition to all the rational and moral
setting of goals during the Enlightenment, Moses Mendelssohn had
"stated that the final objective of all art is beauty, and Karl Philipp
Moritz (1757–93) that 'art exists for its own sake.' " [14]

Thus on the threshold of the Classic era one meets the first in-
timation of the idea of "art for art's sake," which has continuously
accompanied music from that day to this. Oscar Wilde's "All art is
quite useless" says nothing other than what the estheticians of the
closing 18th century were saying. But if, for music, every external
and internal link to aims and uses fell away, did that mean it
should become a purely esoteric play of sound? A mere fretwork
of tracery and arabesques, a sheer pattern of forms? Far from this,
in the Classic age a higher task was allotted to it, particular only to
itself and to be achieved only with its own means: its "serious essential purpose" was to be the embodiment of purest humanity.
With Herder the idea had already taken root that music is the
highest of all the arts because it alone possesses the capacity to lift
man above himself, freed of all the residue of the world of the
senses, into the regions of pure spirit—an idea that appears in
Goethe too, and that was then to be countless times inflected by
the Romantic writers to the point of frenetic enthusiasm. From
now on the music of the late Baroque was often considered a
mere jugglery of sophisticated technique; from Johann Adolf
Scheibe through Christoph Nichelmann, Salomon Sulzer, J. A. P.
Schulz to Gluck and his famous demands, music was summoned
again and again to simplicity, truth, ingenuousness. Herder declared: "How extravagant it can be we know well enough; for a
long, too-long time it has been showing off its juggler's art; what a
new world of serious purposes lies before it!" [15] A "new" world of

14. Goldschmidt, *op. cit.*, p. 173.
15. Wiora, *op. cit.*, p. 128.

"serious" purposes. Never before and probably seldom since was the moral self-portrayal and self-ennobling of man set before music as a guide in such penetrating words. For the first time music is granted the autonomy that releases it from "imitation of Nature," from "diversion of mind and wits," as well as from the role of "handmaiden of theology," and is recognized as a moral force subject to its own laws. "What all the great masters of this 'classical' epoch have in common is the will, out of a sovereign human creative force and an emphatically earthly feeling of life, to animate the material spiritually, to wed *pathos* and *logos,* out of individual human experience to embody in beautiful perfection the universally human, the purely human, as well as in general to elevate to highest perfection the creative powers of the autonomous personality that dictates its own laws in freedom." [16]

Hence everything extravagant or immoderate must fall away; exuberance, superabundance (like Beethoven's and Spontini's, say) becomes repulsive (as it did to Zelter); [17] and concentration of musical expression on wholeness and universal validity through the use of the simplest possible means inevitably become the standard. Where obscurity loses itself in the infinite, and superabundance of means threatens to upset the balance of statement, there "Romanticism," now understood as the antithesis to Classicism, begins to take over in the work of art. "Technique and mechanism intensified to their utmost," as Goethe wrote Eckermann (January 12, 1827), lead composers to the point where "their works no longer remain music; they go beyond the level of human feelings, and to such things one can no longer contribute anything from one's own mind and heart." This much-misunderstood sentence does not imply that Goethe demanded of instrumental music that it offer a visible program. Rather, it contains in a nutshell the whole split between the Classic and Romantic points of view in music: where music makes use of such intensified means that it despotically sweeps the listener under its spell and robs him of his own powers of imagination, it ceases to be "music"—that is, it over-

16. Gerber, *op. cit.,* p. 662.
17. According to Mies, *op. cit.,* p. 433.

steps the boundary of what in the classical sense is allowable. Goethe, to be sure, did not wish to recognize, at least in literature, the difference between the two terms: "What is all this fuss about classic and romantic! The point is that a work should be sound through and through and it will probably be classic as well" (to Eckermann, October 17, 1828). But he was fully aware that "the notion of classic and romantic poetry is spreading over the whole world and causing such quarrels and dissension," that this argument had originally been called forth by his own opposition to Schiller (to Eckermann, March 21, 1830), indeed, that in *Faust* he himself had set the two "poetical forms" of Classicism and Romanticism into "positive relief" (again to Eckermann, December 16, 1829).

The Classic and the Romantic are involved and interwoven with each other in music much as they are in literature, with no possibility of precise separation between them. As early as in the writings of Wilhelm Heinse, Wackenroder, and Tieck—that is, from the 1780s on—it is to be observed that while the task of music is seen to be its own autonomous self-portrayal of man, the character of a sovereign is increasingly pressed upon it, compelling the listener to passive surrender. To the Romanticists it is not what Herder calls "the highest example of coherent order," but rather "beautiful poetic ecstasy," an art "that the darker and more secretive its language, the more universally it agitates all the forces of our being," an art "above mankind," which "depicts human feelings in a superhuman manner," a new religion that "rescues" man from earthly pain, wraps him "with myriad rays . . . in shining clouds" and lifts him up "into the ancient embrace of all-loving Heaven," as Wackenroder puts it in *Berglinger*. Here Goethe clearly dissociated himself from Wackenroder (*Annalen,* 1802); here the Classic parts company with the Romantic. Where the dividing line runs in empirical music is of course a scarcely answerable question. And furthermore: there is basically no boundary line. For this idealistic view of the nature of music is common to both tendencies: from Herder to Pfitzner the autonomy of music in its aims and in its laws has never been put in doubt, any more than

have its humanity and its intrinsic value. Only the emphases are
differently distributed. The determining factors would be inherent
in the symbolic power of form and the spontaneous, fulfilling participation of the listener: music the content of which resides in the
power of an autonomous symbol and which challenges the listener
to participation is felt to be classic. In contradistinction, a music
the formative strength of which is weaker but which for that reason imposes upon the hearer its demonic powers will be found romantic. As Gerber says, "Seen from a considerable distance, the
Classic-Romantic epoch in German music is a unity, because in it
the human being is central, and specifically human emotional values mold the meaning and content of the musical statement. . . .
In the dualisms of law and freedom, of intellect and the senses, of
wholeness and detail, which the classic composer, however differently at different times, was able to reconcile in an equilibrium, the
elements that had been secondary at a given time now win the
upper hand, so that the goal is no longer the universally human,
but the individually human." [18]

18. MGG, article *Deutschland*, section E, 324–25.

III

The Turn to the Classic Period

The beginnings of what music historiography designates as the Classic period reach back to before the middle of the 18th century, into the generation of Johann Sebastian Bach. The start of the Classic-Romantic style period is marked by the determination to simplify all forms and stylistic means, by the deliberate break with the highly intensified composing techniques of the waning Baroque. It is an intentional primitivization such as music history has scarcely experienced at any other time. What Scheibe criticized Bach for, the "artificiality" and "confusion" that obscured "natural beauty," already seemed old-fashioned to the progressive musicians of Bach's own generation (like Telemann, Graupner, Heinichen, and even Handel); what they sought was immediacy of emotional expression through the simplest possible means. Bach, Handel, and Domenico Scarlatti were born in 1685, Telemann four, Graupner and Heinichen two years earlier. Antonio Caldara and Giovanni Bononcini, both born in 1670, belong to a still earlier age-group; Reinhard Keiser was eleven years older than Bach, François Couperin as much as seventeen years older. Even in their generation, minds were divided, some following the leadership of Italy, in part also that of France. There were those who, by preference, clung to inherited views and the Baroque way of thinking; and others—Telemann in his late period perhaps most clearly of all—who had already definitely turned off in the new direction. If one attempted to pursue the pre-history of Classicism in music still further back, it would presumably split up into separate national tendencies; the subject has as yet not been investigated. In the next generation—that of Quantz, Hasse, Karl Hein-

rich Graun, Giovanni Battista Sammartini, Tartini, Giovanni Platti
—and even more so in that of Bach's sons, to which belong
among others Domenico Alberti, Pergolesi, Galuppi, Stamitz, Wagenseil, and so forth—the endeavor to produce a music that should
be "beautiful, moving, impressive, and noble," to quote Scheibe,
was common to all composers, no matter what their artistic and
national origin.

With this challenge melody moves into the foreground as the
sustaining and basic element; melodic theory is a principal concern
of musicians from Scheibe and Nichelmann on, until, significantly,
at the beginning of the 19th century harmonic theory becomes the
primary and fundamental branch of study (according to Heinrich
Christoph Koch). For the first time in history the beauty of a
piece is decided no longer by the concurrence of more or less
equal voices linked together in the composition, but by the unrestricted sovereignty of the melody, which is not overshadowed by
obbligato contrapuntal or "concertizing" voices, but "accompanied" now by a quite simple substructure that is not obbligato and
can be left out. It is indicative that Haydn, even in his old age, is
reported to have said, "If you want to know whether a melody is
really beautiful, sing it without accompaniment." Here we have a
rejection of vast import. What had been built up in all periods and
style-phases of music history and despite all modifications had still
been considered fundamental, what Bach had once again laid
down in the "esoteric handicraft" of his late *Kunstbücher* (his para-
digmatic works, such as the *Art of Fugue*)—in final concentration and refinement—this is precisely what was now rejected with
determination. It was really an epochal turn of widest range. This
decision is not to be compared with the call to do battle against
counterpoint issued around 1600 by a few revolutionary Florentine
enthusiasts of Antiquity. There the concern had been only to experiment in setting a new style alongside one already evolved, a *seconda* beside a *prima pratica* the continued existence of which was
not questioned.[19] Here, however, a complete break was involved

19. Friedrich Blume, *Renaissance and Baroque Music,* New York, 1967,
p. 117 ff.

and a (supposedly) lasting rejection of all old categories, forms, and stylistic means, the dethroning of reason in favor of the heart and the setting up of a musical fairyland of simple and engaging beauty.

That doing this meant taking a revolutionary step of the greatest consequence, those who took it were well aware. The feeling of standing at an important parting of the ways was everywhere; Johann Samuel Petri, in the second edition (1782) of his *Anleitung zur praktischen Musik,* spoke of "the great catastrophe in music." Depending on their personal attitudes, musicians made fun of this "easy melody-making" (Marpurg) or shed tears over the languorous sensation of a "melting portamento" (Schubart). But more farseeing spirits recognized that music could not be supported by this new art of melody alone. The sense of being on the verge of losing a great heritage, without really knowing what to put in its place, spread a veil of discontent, and there was no trace, as this era of sentiment began, of the "optimistic enthusiasm" with which the Baroque had started off. To be sure, restless individuals enthusiastically demolished the "inflated pomposity" of the past, but there was little question of a naïve faith in continuous further development of music to ever greater heights.

At the start of the Classic period there appeared rather a certain timorous resignation, a sense of the futility of private sentiment before the decaying grandeur of a powerful past. The health of all of the older music was thought to have sprung from the sung epics and ballads of a graying past and from the naturalistic immediacy of folksong; after Thomas Percy, with his *Reliques of Ancient English Poetry* (1765), and James Macpherson, with his "Ossian" poems (from 1760 on), had drawn attention to the beauty of supposedly ancient folksong-poetry, the deterioration of folksong was often looked upon as the cause of the decline.[20]

"We are living on the ruins: what will the singers of heroic poems and the minor comedy-writers and makers of little tunes have to say now?" "The remnants of the old folk way of thinking," wrote Herder, "are rolling with a hastening final rush into the

20. Cf. Wiora, *op. cit.,* p. 74 ff., p. 120 ff.

abyss of the past"; people are content with "composed trivialities
of the most common sort"; "together with genuine folksong, the
basis of all poetry . . . is being murdered." Not by "easy melody-
making" but only by "genuine folksong" can the deteriorating
music of the West be restored to health. Out of this wellspring
composers can find the way to bring about a renewal. Gluck in his
"folk-born simplicity" was able to do this, and the result is, Herder
goes on to say, that "most of the arias in his opera *Orpheus* are as
plain and simple as those of the English ballads." One will have to
ponder along what lines a music will still be possible in the future
that is not idly playful, nor boring, nor amusing, nor utilitarian,
but is able to attain that high aim of raising man out of and beyond himself, that consummate humanity and dignity whose image
hovers before all great minds. Herder recognized that from now on
the composer would have the choice of three ways: thoughtless
riding-ahead in artificialities that had long since grown hollow, "in
entertainments without content or essence"; or a return to the past
(that is, a deliberate revivification of historic models long left behind); or, again, a rebirth from the spirit of genuine folk music.

It was not only Herder who thought this; the same view recurs
in Schiller (in his review of Bürger's poems) and Goethe (his review of von Arnim and Brentano's collection of German songs,
Des Knaben Wunderhorn), as it does later in Schumann, Robert
Franz, and countless others; it comes to the surface on repeated
occasions during the Romantic period (despite all artiness); and it
finally enjoyed a late resurrection in the musical Youth Movement
of the 1920s in Germany. The three ways that Herder saw in fact
determined the whole course of the Classic-Romantic period: the
continued "riding along" (even if Herder did find it "thoughtless")
in the forms of the late Baroque; the historicity reaching back into
the depths of the past and thence again and again providing models for individual creativity; and—the most fruitful and really genuine creative possibility—the self-renewal from folk music. All three
ideas are ready to hand at the beginning of the Classic period and
have accompanied the Classic-Romantic period up to the present
time.

If we regard these ideas as basic to Classic-Romantic music, we come to the conclusion that this epoch in music history had not yet reached an end even by the middle of the 20th century. The continued "carrying on" nevertheless led to the rescue and transfer from the Baroque of all the church-music categories—Mass, motet, church cantata, and chorale arrangements in their various forms—and of oratorio, opera, and many other kinds of music, to be recast in the new style. Counterpoint and fugue, scorned at first, were preserved and renewed to become pillars of Classic-Romantic style. Historicism, from A. F. J. Thibaut's Palestrina cult on, resulted in the revival of old and still older music and, in connection therewith, in historical musicology itself; from this activity an infinite number of stimuli inspired composers of the 19th and 20th centuries, and the end of this historicism in the creative activity of our times is not yet foreseeable. But perhaps the most important change—and a true stroke of good fortune—is the fact that the musicians of the Classic-Romantic period instinctively and without theoretical speculations drew their nourishment from folksong (even though folksong is here to be understood in the broadest sense of the term, from the medieval chant to the opera arietta). For now fresh blood flowed into the shaping of Western music, and certainly the most lasting achievement of the Classic-Romantic period of music history lies in the blending of folk elements with the highest art of composition.

IV

The Nations, "Mixed Taste," and the "Universal Language"

It is somewhat surprising that at the start of the Classic era no new nation immediately took a commanding lead—as the Netherlanders, for instance, had done at the start of the Renaissance, and the Italians at that of the Baroque. Instead, the turn to the Classic period had been begun by musicians who were themselves Italian or at least Italian-trained. In the hands of composers like Attilio Ariosti, Bononcini, Handel, Caldara, Hasse, Graun, and so forth, opera seria had been widely preparing the ground for the rising new sense of style; this was even more the case with the intermezzo and opera buffa of the Pergolesis, the Leonardo Vincis, etc., while Italian oratorio had already firmly taken on early Classic features.

Italian opera, oratorio, solo cantata, and related compositions beyond a doubt smoothed the way for the change of style, but so also did instrumental categories like the orchestral opera-sinfonia. For other categories of instrumental music the process was similar. Independently of each other, Italian, French, and German composers effected the turn to the new style. In the generation preceding Joseph Haydn, however, an extremely rapid and successful advance took place in the new German instrumental music in all its categories, to the point of setting up a German hegemony that brought with it a profound alteration in the national structure of European music. The Italian period of the Baroque was replaced by the German Classic-Romantic period. If one places the beginning of this period at around 1740, with the coming into prominence of Bohemian composers in the musical capitals of various countries, with the development of the early Viennese school around Wagenseil and the North German school around Philipp Emanuel Bach, it becomes clear that German music—instrumental music, at least, but also not insignificantly vocal music, even opera —had achieved an unprecedented world validity, a world validity that held throughout the 19th century and has gradually diminished only since about 1910.

The importance of the Italian composers was in no way curtailed by this development; on the contrary, even with the passing of the Italian hegemony their vigor was still great enough for them to prepare the transition into the new, a fact that bears notable witness to their creative capacity. That masters like Sammartini, Niccolò Jommelli, Domenico Scarlatti, Alberti, Galuppi, Platti, Tartini, and later Pergolesi established the point of departure for the Classic piano sonata, symphony, string quartet, etc. (a point to which in France such composers as Jean Marie Leclair, Gabriel Guillemain, Jean-Joseph de Mondonville, and Jean-Pierre Guignon go back) is just as unquestionable as that the categories of Classic instrumental music did not grow out of any single school at any single place but evolved gradually from the various concurrent and interweaving tendencies. Hugo Riemann too one-sidedly regarded the Mannheim school as the source, as Guido Adler did the Viennese school and Fausto Torrefranca the Italian. Joseph Haydn cannot be ascribed to any school, and the greatness of his achievement is due in considerable part to his sovereign autonomy. Moreover, Italy in the first place, France in the second, continued throughout the entire Classic period to produce models and incentives. Without French opera, both Gluck and Beethoven's *Fidelio* are equally inconceivable; Mozart offers the ultimate example of continuous assimilation of frequently changing models from both countries as well as from the various German schools. The Italian opera composers, from Alessandro Scarlatti on to Cimarosa and Paisiello, to Donizetti and Bellini, catered to the European stage far more than the German composers did and, with Rossini, one of their most fascinating composers in the Classic period, exercised a quite un-

limited command over the theater of all Europe, much as Verdi
was to do in the Romantic phase.

But the whole historical picture is not altered hereby: the Classic-Romantic period is the great (perhaps the first great?) period
of instrumental music. In this field, from the middle of the 18th
century to the beginning of the 20th, German composers and prac-
titioners of music occupied a position of undisputed pre-eminence
in all European music centers, and as teachers, virtuosos, conductors, and directors, as well as composers, took a leading part in the
cultivation of music all over the world. Aftereffects of this situation
are still to be traced in the role of Germans among the stars of
modern conducting. Haydn's symphonies and oratorios are among
the first masterpieces of European music to have been performed
in America (by around 1800). From Haydn to Beethoven (for the
Classic era in the narrower sense) and on through the entire Romantic phase up to Richard Strauss, the picture has not essentially
changed despite the increasing self-reliance and international activity of other countries. From Forkel to Riemann, Abert, Schering,
and others, German musicology, too, stood at the top. Though the
conservatories in Paris and St. Petersburg—not to speak of the
many Italian schools—led their own lives, even they could not escape the influence of the German centers of musical education, not
only in Europe but also in the New World. It is therefore not un-
justified to see in the Classic era and on through the Classic-Romantic period an epoch of German music, at least in the sense that
German musicians provided a standard, sometimes the determining
contribution to the world's musical culture, creativity, and education.

Paris, London, St. Petersburg, at times Rome, Milan, Press-
burg, Prague, Brussels, Amsterdam, and many other music centers
in foreign countries near and far became the temporary domain of
German musicians. In this the Bohemians at first took an extensive
part; it is not yet possible to distinguish between their German and
their Czechish contributions. Paris was a center of German music.
Here Baron von Grimm was able to play a decisive role at times as
arbiter and reporter; here Gluck experienced his hardest battles and

his greatest triumphs; here Nicholas Étienne Framery in 1770 (in his *Réflexions*) expressly recognized the leadership of German music. In Paris, by 1744, Franz Xaver Richter received a license for printing his music. In 1751 a symphony was performed for the first time at the Concerts Spirituels; Stamitz himself had appeared there as virtuoso in 1748. The symphony as the typical genre of German music was here called *"sinfonie d'Allemagne,"* the horns, which typically lend it its color, appear as *"cors allemands."* Bayard the publisher put out a collection of symphonies under the title of *La Melodia Germanica.* In Paris, as well as in Amsterdam, Brussels, London, and so on, great quantities of German instrumental music appeared in print. In connection with the proliferation of this music, the business of music publishing took an undreamt-of upward swing in Germany and other countries. From this fruitful soil, subsequently important firms, like Artaria in Vienna, André in Offenbach, Schott in Mainz, Pleyel in Paris, Clementi in London, Bossler in Speyer, Hummel in Amsterdam—and many less long-lived houses like Mollo, Imbault, Sieber, Boyer and Le Menu, Nägeli, Birchall, Forster, Longman & Broderip—not to mention Simrock in Bonn, Hoffmeister (Bureau de Musique, later to become C. F. Peters), and Breitkopf & Härtel in Leipzig, grew great.

As in all epochs of music history, in the course of time other countries advanced into prominence with their own typical production. This was not yet the case, however, in the Classic phase (in the narrower sense); only in the last third of the 19th century did the Russians, Poles, Hungarians, Bohemians (from now on definitely Czechish in national character), and after mid-century the Scandinavians come forward with characteristic contributions. France, after the advent of Impressionism, became particularly influential. In the Classic phase itself the picture remained essentially unchanged.

With how little self-confidence the Germans originally approached their historic task is best shown by the singular doctrine of "mixed taste" (*vermischter Geschmack*) represented primarily by Quantz and with some variation by Leopold Mozart and C. P. E.

Bach. According to Quantz (*Versuch,* 1752) two peoples "deserve credit for the improvement in musical taste in recent times," the Italians and the French. All writers of the time distinguish emphatically between Italian, French, and German musical style. Herder still clung to this approach [21] and even in Goethe a similar distinction is to be found. Italian music was praised for its expressive power, its sensuousness, its tender singing character, its wealth of inspiration; French music for its vivacity, especially in rhythm, its pleasing quality and easy accessibility—though it was censured for its dryness and its schematic cast. From far back the Germans had inherited the advantages of solid compositional craft and instrumental virtuosity; "but of good taste and of beautiful melodies one finds, save for a few old church songs, few indications. . . . They try to compose artfully rather than comprehensibly or pleasingly, more for the eye than for the ear." On the other hand, Quantz grants the Germans a particular ability to "assimilate other peoples' tendencies in taste, whichever they may wish"; they "know how to make use of what is good in all sorts of foreign music." A mixing of style is therefore recommended to them as a recipe for arriving at a music "that will be accepted by many countries and recognized as good." Quantz does not hesitate to characterize such a "mixed taste" as "the present German taste."

This fitted in with widely held views. Telemann had already boasted of being able to compose in any style. Mozart reported from Mannheim (February 7, 1778) that he was able "to adopt and imitate almost all sorts and styles of composition." Yet this remarkable tendency only goes to show how the German musicians saw themselves and their tradition and how they were trying to justify their own anti-traditional doings. What they achieved was, after a brief period of transition, anything but a blending of styles. They were, far rather, creating out of their own specifically German talent something fundamentally new, however much of other national stylistic traditions may have been absorbed into it, and were raising this something new to a wholly unprecedented height of musical statement.

21. Wiora, *op. cit.,* p. 118 ff.

The Classic period itself set its aims considerably higher than Quantz and his contemporaries had suspected. Composers very soon realized that the purpose of their efforts could not be the coining of a new national style alongside existing styles, or making foreign national styles their own; that it was far more a matter of creating something above and beyond national styles, something of worldwide validity, a "universal language" of music in which all peoples, without distinction, and all levels of society too, could take part—a language of humanity. This humanistic idea arose in German music simultaneously with the similarly-directed idea in German literature. Gluck (in a letter to the "Mercure de France," February, 1773) [22] declared that he wished to write "a strong music that speaks to the heart," that would "appeal to all peoples" and "wipe out the ridiculous differences in national music." Chabanon praised Gluck's late style as "the universal language of our continent" (*De la musique,* 1785). For Herder music is simply "an art of mankind"; it humanizes the human race.[23] This is the meaning, too, that lies behind Haydn's famous remark: "My language is understood in the whole world." It is the spiritual concept of music that ultimately culminates in the composition of Schiller's *Ode to Joy,* and in Beethoven's Ninth Symphony. Yet one should not fail to note that with Beethoven, beginning at the time of the Heiligenstadt testament, this concept persisted in perpetual contradiction to that other concept which saw in music mainly the expression of the individual self, the statement of what lay in a person's inmost heart, the outlet for the pressure of unbearable torments and discords of soul—in short, a frankly romantic evaluation of music. One may see (though only for Beethoven himself) the period from the Heiligenstadt testament (October 6, 1802) to the completion of the Ninth Symphony (1824) as a time in which Classic and Romantic views of music met in continual opposition.

The striving for a universal language makes it possible to understand the remarkable fact that, along with all the increase in

22. Reprinted in Oliver Strunk, ed., *Source Readings in Music History,* New York, 1950, pp. 681–83 (or paperback ed., *Source Readings . . . The Classical Era,* New York, 1965, pp. 107–09).
23. Wiora, *op. cit.,* p. 83 ff.

musical technique and artistic means that began with Sammartini, Platti, Johann Christoph Wagenseil, and Stamitz and reached its final height in Beethoven, there always ran a tendency toward the simple, the generally comprehensible, the folklike. It does not come to light in every work nor in every composer, is even quite deserted at times (as in Beethoven's last string quartets), but everywhere breaks through again unconcealed. It brings about the assimilation of countless folksong melodies and popular elements, the leaning upon dance, song, march, the intentional implication of the popular (the "illusion of the familiar" in J. A. P. Schulz's *Lieder "im Volkston,"* 1782 and later), the many quotations from German or foreign folksongs, and the borrowing of folk melodies as themes for variations (as is so often the case with Haydn and Beethoven). It finally produces, in history's lucky moments, a music that succeeds in being at once to the highest degree popular and in the highest measure consummate art (*The Magic Flute, The Creation, The Seasons*). This goal, of a universal language that embraces all humanity and erases all differences in station and culture, was often attained, if ever in music history, at the zenith of the Classic period between Gluck's *Orfeo* (1762) and Schubert's *Schöne Müllerin* (1823), and although it was by no means always striven for, was most purely realized in exactly those works that represented highest achievements. This endeavor fundamentally distinguishes the Classic era not only from the Baroque, in which folk music had not yet counted for anything, but also from several later Romantic tendencies (Neo-Germanism and Impressionism, for example) in which it no longer counted at all. Goethe's idea that the folksong revitalized in his own day could now be lost again if it had "accomplished its mission" of "eliciting new significant melodies" (as he put it in his review of *Des Knaben Wunderhorn*) was fulfilled in a different and far more fruitful manner than he had foreseen—in the highest achievements of the Viennese Classics.

V

The Classic Style
and Its Phases

Composers of the Classic era worked hard to achieve a style adequate to the expression of their ideas. The genetic history of this style may be divided into two phases, an early Classic, which extends from the beginnings into the 1770s and includes the so-called *style galant* and style of "sensibility" (*Empfindsamkeit*), and a High Classic, in which forms and stylistic means remained basically constant (grammar and syntax of the universal language had been developed, so to speak) and composers were in a position to shape ideas that sprang from their free imagination in a fully evolved language, according to their personal capacity. The elementary forms of the style were all fashioned in the early Classic phase; seen from the point of view of style history, the High Classic phase brought their further development only in the distinctive modes of speech of the individual masters. In music historiography the High Classic phase goes by the name of "Viennese Classic" for two reasons: because its leading representatives worked in Vienna (or Austria) and because a specifically Viennese (or Austrian) element passed into the Classic style. From Haydn to Brahms and beyond, the "Viennese style" remained one of the chief foundation stones of the German musical language.

The *style galant* is often regarded as a sort of postlude to the Baroque and set on a par with the Rococo in the plastic arts. The parallel is close, for in the painting and decorative arts of the Rococo a fanciful grace is met with, a "sfumato," a languishing delicacy, but also an irony and a melancholy—all qualities similar to those in many a musical composition in the *style galant,* particularly in its "sensibility" phase. But this parallel, aside from being scarcely tenable on chronological grounds, overlooks the fact that Rococo forms in the plastic arts emerged directly from the late Baroque forms, whereas in music the *style galant* comes toward the end of the gap separating the younger period from the older: the intentional limitation of means, the precious ingenuousness, and the priority of monodic melody with only incidental accompaniment make it clear that the basic feeling governing the *style galant* is far rather Classic than Baroque. The Rococo of the plastic arts, to be sure, is not exactly separated by a gap from its Classic style but often absorbed "classicistic" traits; the *galant* style in music, however, goes straight through its "sensibility stage" (as Gerber calls it) into a sort of *Sturm und Drang* interlude and thence into the High Classic phase. In other words: the "sensibility" style, the *Sturm und Drang,* and the High Classic in music are by no means to be defined as contrasts to the *galant* style, whereas the "classicism" of the plastic arts *is* a contrast to the Rococo. Contemporary title-pages of opera librettos and printed music as well as portraits of musicians speak clearly to this point; they are marked by the sober clarity of classic design far more than by baroque excitement. Hence one will do well to incorporate the *style galant* into the Classic period as an early stage. To attempt a basic differentiation between it, the "sensibility" style, and *Sturm und Drang* is not possible. What as a rule is called "sensible" (*empfindsam*) is only the greater emphasis on elements expressive of sentiment in the *style galant,* and beyond that *Sturm und Drang* is a short-lived movement that passes from the idyllic playing with sentiments into the sphere of the great passions before all this is transfigured in the High Classic stage into expression of the universally human.

A] RHYTHM, METER, TEMPO

Perhaps the clearest evidence of the change in style lies in the novelty of rhythmic and metrical elements in early Classic music. Here, too, there are transitions; here, too, it is often hard to draw a boundary line: in their rhythm and their meter Rameau, Domenico Scarlatti, and Handel show features now still Baroquish, now more Classic. Yet very early, what was later to dominate the entire Classic-Romantic period begins to become a fundamental law: periodic meter and differentiated rhythm. Roughly speaking, the late Baroque knew no regularly recurrent periodic structures. In all the exacting forms and categories like fugues, ricercars, and also sonata movements, arias, choruses, etc., such structures are quite deliberately avoided. They are naturally most likely to be found in dances and dancelike types, but even there composers are inclined to veil the regularity, to enlarge the periods by means of melodic extensions, to place cadences irregularly or to bypass them, thus preventing any feeling of a simple left-right or heavy-light order. Every analysis of Bach or Handel suites and concerto movements confirms this; where actually danced dances are concerned (as in the stage ballet), the periodic simplicity is of course more evident. For the late Baroque composer an important means of veiling the periodic framework (in so far as it is present at all) is provided by the rhythm running uniformly throughout a piece, to some extent making orientation more difficult for the listener and preventing the rise of any feeling of regularly recurring beats and accents. Quite otherwise with early Classic composition, which simply takes folk dance and folksong for its model and (axiomatically) strives for the unambiguous regularity of eight-measure periodicity. Indicative of this is the change of the Baroque minuet into the Classic minuet: beat and meter remain (the Baroque minuet, too, inclines toward simple and accented periodicity), but what bears the name of minuet in the Classic period is frequently a folk dance—like the ländler, the zwiefacher (a Bavarian dance), and such—and with Schubert at times almost a waltz; until finally (even as early as Haydn) these turn more and more into characteristic pieces without specifically dancelike traits. In countless compositions of the early Classic phase (songs, piano pieces, chamber-music movements, but also opera arias, choruses, etc.) whether one turns to Platti or to Rameau, to Wagenseil or to Hasse, one finds the simplicity of this construction elevated to the level of a law. Stamitz and his compa-

triots often go about it in an almost tiresome and primitive manner. The period is as a rule subdivided in four- and two-measure
motifs and this is not infrequently carried out so baldly that one
has the impression of a chopped-up patchwork of small-jointed
bits and pieces, no less in Haydn's and even in Mozart's earliest
works than with minor masters like Josef Schuster, Johann Samuel
Schröter, *et al.* Then in the High Classic phase Heinrich Christoph
Koch (in his *Versuch einer Anleitung zur Komposition,* 1782–93)
expressly laid down the eight-measure period as a basic principle.

Things naturally did not remain at this primitive level. In the
High Classic era, periodic structure became more complicated.
Haydn and especially Mozart often write, with utmost delicacy and
the finest sense of proportion, periods that appear to consist of
eight measures but are often quite irregularly built, and they
change the periodic structure within a movement. A good part of
the lively and energetic effect produced by their works (especially
in their later years) lies in this alternation between variously constructed periods and in the refinement of inner tension that bal-
ances such irregularly built periods into an apparent regularity.
Herein lies, too, a good part of the distinction between the great
masters and their lesser contemporaries, who missed this sensitivity
to tension and balance within the period as the nucleus of the composition. Dittersdorf, Dussek, and others often enough rode the
eight-measure period to death. Beethoven's sense of periodicity,
which Riemann sought to clarify in his analyses, is often very irregular, arbitrary, even ambiguous. In him there already begins to
show a certain striving to conceal the classicity of a clear and easily followed periodic structure by means of fragmentation and cor-
rosion (e.g. the C♯ minor string Quartet, Op. 131, fifth movement); for which purpose he once more goes back to continuous
rhythm, prohibited and avoided since the late Baroque, which
makes orientation more difficult (e.g. the E♭ String Quartet, Op.
127, Finale, Allegro commodo). It was Beethoven who resisted
the iron clamp of regular periodicity far more strongly than his
younger contemporaries and his followers. His frequent breaking
through of this structure is certainly one of the causes that made

his works (especially the late ones) so difficult for these people to understand. In doing this he also broke one of the fundamental tenets of the Classic style: to make a composition easily accessible to the listener for his co-operation in its fulfillment. It was just the so-called Romantics, on the other hand, who returned much more frequently to simplicity in their periodic structure: Weber, Schubert, Marschner, and many others, as well as Schumann and Brahms—and Wagner not excepted—did not hesitate to pay homage to the eight-measure period; Bruckner often noted the number of measures (representing the periodic structure) in the margin of his manuscript scores.

If a basic principle of construction had been found in the eight-measure period (the origin of which without doubt lies in the music of dance, song, and march) and therewith a stylistic means opening the way to a universal language, then rhythm, against this background, could be differentiated in endless gradations without endangering comprehensibility. In the Classic era, rhythm came to support refinement of expression. In contrast to the homogeneous (motor) rhythm of the late Baroque there is to be noticed everywhere among the early Classic composers a tendency to broken, if also individually stereotyped, rhythms. Dotted rhythms, Lombard rhythms (Scotch snap), syncopations, recitative-like rubatos, the gentlest transitions and often richly nuanced gradations (as in Wilhelm Friedemann and Philipp Emanuel Bach) are to be observed alongside sturdy dance and march rhythms; certain ways of alternating two- and three-note figures and triplet cadences simply became the fashion.

While the late Baroque loved having all upper voices take part in articulating the even continuity of rhythm or assigning its own continuous rhythm to each upper voice over a bass that progresses evenly or in rhythmic ostinato, basses were now often confined to stereotyped functions, more or less without profile, of marking the beat and defining the motion, while the melody-bearing top voice is distinguished by a strongly differentiated rhythm, variable, often nervous, and fascinating. If there is a second melodic voice, in the early Classic stage it often definitely withdraws behind the first (as, for example, in the trio sonata, in contrast to the "classic"—in this case the Baroque—trio sonata). The Italian composers lean toward a vital, often thrashing rhythm, the French toward precise and stereotyped rhythm; Bohemian and Austrian musicians are fond of dancelike, swinging, springy, sauntering, comfortable, or even sentimental motion. All of them make a point of rhythmic design that is energetic, lively, vigorous, or feelingly nuanced, but in any case strongly differentiated.

In the High Classic period this sort of treatment reached an ever greater refinement as independence of the voices in the texture increased with the development of what Riemann called the *durchbrochen* ("filigree") style. In instrumental movements for trio, quartet, quintet, in the ensembles of opera or Mass, this is carried in Haydn, Mozart, and Beethoven to a subtle collaboration of more or less similar, divergent, even contrasting rhythms, so highly cultivated that it is not surpassed, often not even equaled, in the late Romantic period. Herewith rhythm in the High Classic period loses its overexcited activity, becomes more "natural," more earthy; Haydn from the 1780s on and Mozart in his late works often attain a polished simplicity of movement (as in melody) that was lacking in the early Classic phase as well as in their own beginnings. Not only melodically but rhythmically, too, their connection with folk music becomes clearest at this time, and that not only in the songs and ariettas of *The Magic Flute* and *The Seasons,* but also in symphonies and string quartets. In contrast, Beethoven's rhythm in the beginning is sometimes part clumsy, part exaggeratedly virtuoso, later often excited and (from the Classic viewpoint) unbridled. In this, too, the early Romantics returned to simpler conditions, while the late Romantics link up again with Beethoven's turbulent and passionate rhythms. It is significant, however, that really new rhythmic formations do not enter the stream of Romanticism until the rise of Russian, Bohemian, Hungarian, and Scandinavian national music.

In the High Classic era, rhythm became an element of composition that made possible greater refinement of expression. Originality of invention is often so stamped upon a rhythmic motif that it just cannot be reused. No composer would have dared, for example, to use again the main rhythmic motif of Beethoven's Fifth Symphony; it would have been like plagiarism. In this respect a step had been taken along the road to individualism that basically ran counter to the nature of the Classic era. By coining original rhythmic motifs composers of the Romantic phase often gave a work a unique and unrepeatable character; some, like Brahms and Bruckner, evolved a sort of personal rhythmic style.

In the music of the late Baroque specific tempo indications were still rare. Since categories and forms were typical, tempos were automatically understood. Where tempo indications do appear, they often call for departures from the norm, unusually slow or fast tempos, changes of tempo within a movement, and the like. With the early Classic period such indications became the rule. The gamut of terms still employed today, from Largo and Adagio to Presto, came rapidly into use. If in the early Classic phase moderate tempos predominate (Allegro, Andante, Allegretto), strongly contrasting, even extreme tempos are frequently (though by no means always) preferred in the High Classic. The Moderato of many of Haydn's opening movements, the Adagio of many of his slow movements, stand in strong contrast to the frequent Prestos of his finales. Beethoven especially is fond of exploiting extreme contrasts (e.g. the Ninth Symphony); his irresistible verve leads him to the *ritmo di tre battute,* the measure loses its individual value and becomes merely an element in larger rhythmic-metrical structures.

Tempo now also serves to characterize, to individualize. Though late Baroque movements admit of considerable latitude in choice of tempo without endangering their character, the early Classic sonata or symphony has already become more sensitive to "wrong" tempos. Haydn movements can be distorted by a poor choice of tempo, Beethoven compels the performer to an absolute tempo by means of very accurate indications (often metronomic). Most difficult are Mozart's late works (though he is the one who uses moderate rather than extreme tempos, and often he does not mark them exactly): the least mistake in choosing a tempo can distort a movement unbearably. It is not by chance that selection of the "right" tempo is regarded as one of the most ticklish and most important problems of the conductor today.

Rate of speed, form of motion, and the over-all structure, together with melodic and harmonic invention, constitute an indestructible unity. In this unity are based the unique, the not-to-be-repeated, compelling, fascinating characteristics of expression the composer has put into his work. But in this unity lies also the constant drive toward what is individual and original. In other words: the Classic is steadily on its way to the Romantic.

B] HARMONY AND TONALITY

In the late Baroque the circle of the twenty-four possible major and minor keys had been fully opened up, at least for keyboard instruments; they had always been accessible to string instruments, and only to the extent that wind instruments were used was it necessary to make adjustments according to their technical possibilities. Even so, composers seldom moved further in the series than A major (F♯ minor) and E♭ major (C minor). Surprisingly enough, however, early Classic composers laid the same or even narrower restrictions upon their choice of keys; never in the history of music were so many pieces written in D, F, G, and B♭. Since this is to be observed not only in orchestral music but in piano and chamber music and the song as well, the reason must be sought not in the playing technique of the instruments but in a deliberate effort at simplicity; simplicity of tonality would surely have been as much a part of a universal language, close to the people, as simplicity of meter and of structure. In striking contrast to the Baroque is the strong preference for major. From the beginnings through to the end of Haydn and Mozart (in Haydn's case save for a period around 1770), pieces in minor are the exception, minor being reserved for rarer spheres of expression. This, too, is to be traced back to the trend toward the smooth and easily understood, but also to the trend toward the bright and cheerful that is especially typical for the early Classic era.

In the transition to the High Classic era, the range of tonalities used broadened significantly. In this Haydn led the way with his middle symphonies (of 1768–72: Nos. 39, 44–46, 49, and 52) and with some of his piano sonatas and string quartets; keys like F♯ major or B major offered no technical difficulties for the orchestra (horns in both keys are called for). While early Classic composers also exercised the greatest reserve in modulation within the movement (development sections like those of Schobert are an exception), with Haydn particularly and still more so with Mozart the modulatory potential quickly spread to the extremes of the possible. The technique of chromatic and enharmonic modulation was exploited in all its ramifications up to the time of Beethoven. Mozart's late works (the last symphonies, string quartets, string quintets) achieve the utmost boldness in linking keys. The young Beethoven at first shrank back in alarm before all this; only in his later works is the richest use again made of modulation.

From the point of view of harmony as well, the early Classic period began with a definite turn away from the highly developed variety of the late Baroque. Composition, especially with the Italians but also with the Bohemians and South Germans, now rests chiefly upon the basic functions of tonic, dominant, and subdominant. Rameau's many writings (among them *Traité de l'harmonie,* 1722; *Démonstration du principe de l'harmonie,* 1750) most clearly reflect the newly awakened feeling for harmony and its limitations; the early Classic composers were very restrained in their use of harmonic means. The products of all tendencies and schools from, say, 1740 to 1760 are totally different from Bach's immense harmonic wealth. This explains why to this period Bach seemed so remote but to the Romantics was immediately convincing: his bold chromatic and enharmonic harmony, so rich in dissonance, came very close to the Romantics' own requirements, for which reason, too, the latter generation no longer had any relationship with the composers of the early Classic. To contemporaries of Scheibe, Hasse, Graun, *et al.,* Bach's harmony appeared grandiloquent, overladen, thick, artificial; to those of Beethoven, Schubert, Weber —to say nothing of later composers—the music of the Grauns, Wagenseils, Stamitzes, and the rest must have seemed empty and poor. At all times esthetic judgment is largely determined by harmonic awareness and feeling. Rameau's system builds on the three basic functions, and for the first time elevates harmony to a theoretical level as a fundament of all composition. The building elements of harmony are the triads. The major and the minor triad are antitheses with their own definite expressive qualities. Simple tonalities correspond to simple feelings, the more remote ones—hence seldom used and to be dealt with sparingly by the composer—to rarer feelings; they should be employed for agitated, dramatic, painful, or otherwise particularly emotional expression. From this point on, a new evaluation of tonalities takes place which departs from the Baroque theory of affective keys; upon it rest, for example, Schubart's and E. T. A. Hoffmann's characterizations of keys. Chromaticisms, used harmonically as well as melodically, become the means of conveying smoothly flowing changes in feeling. The authentic cadence is the chief means of articulation; the plagal cadence, the deceptive cadence, and others take on the significance of secondary articulatory elements dependent on the expression. To this the early Classic practice altogether corresponds with its sparing use of the more remote tonalities, subsidiary cadences, chromaticism, and modulation to distant keys. In the North German composers, especially in Wilhelm Friedemann and Philipp Emanuel Bach, complicated harmonic relationships still survive from the preceding period; and it was probably from Philipp Emanuel Bach via Haydn that they rejoined the mainstream in the High Classic period.

In response to the differentiated requirements of the High Classic period, then, harmony once again became more strongly differentiated. Herein, too, the great masters are distinguished from their lesser contemporaries. While, for example, Dittersdorf, Francesco Antonio Rosetti (Franz Anton Rössler), Pleyel, and others cling to a simple treatment in basic functions with occasional modulations, Haydn in his later years turns not infrequently to harmonic intensifications and complications in the form of unexpected modulations and harmonic contrasts. The much-discussed "surprises" of his finales are often achieved by sudden diversion into

quite unexpected keys (that they were brought about through a
trick—as for instance in the finale of Symphony No. 100, by an
apparently erroneous step into a "false" key—had the effect on his
contemporaries of a joke, a witticism, and brought many a rebuke
upon his head). Mozart's works differ from Haydn's later ones essentially by their much greater wealth of chromatic and dissonant
effects, their preference for unusual tonalities and unexpected modulations—above all in that their changes of key always bring with
them a profound change in the expressive sphere (for example, the
modulation from C to D♭ in the Andante of the String Quartet, K.
387, that from E♭ minor to E major in the Adagio of the String
Quintet, K. 516, that from A♭ major to B minor in the Andante of
the Symphony, K. 543). In addition there are the countless sudden
harmonic evasions and shifts, the sudden "cloudings-over" (e.g. in
the Andante of the Symphony, K. 543, the rapid shadow cast as
A♭ moves to its minor) that many times lend his late works the
"romantic" charm of something intangible, yearning, nocturnal, or
remote and that are a chief means in the service of his variety of
expression.

Beethoven in his early days is much simpler, more direct, and
subsequently often more monumental, more "exalted," but also
rougher (cf. his turn to D♭ in the C major Largo of his Piano Sonata, Op. 7, of 1796–97, with the same turn in the Andante of
Mozart's String Quartet, K. 387, of 1782: what in Mozart is understood as shadowy remoteness and secret, far-off sound, has in
Beethoven, because of the preceding modulation into A♭, rather
the effect of mitigating the deep seriousness that reigns throughout
the movement). This also holds for the famous turn to D♭ in the
Adagio of the Ninth Symphony. Otherwise the harmony in Beethoven's late works is often very ragged and abrupt; rapid changes
of key, digressive shifts, often only brief but violent in effect, are
linked with piled-up chromatic and enharmonic effects (as in the
Adagio of the Piano Sonata in B♭, Op. 106, of 1817–18),
brusque contrasts are heaped one upon the other in titanic fashion
(as in the third movement, the *Heiliger Dankgesang,* of the String
Quartet in A minor, Op. 132).

Mozart's harmony as well as Beethoven's prepared the way well in advance for the Romantic composers; Schubert in this respect links up rather with Mozart, Berlioz clearly with Beethoven. But with the harmony of Beethoven and Mozart the field had in truth been exhausted and what the German Romantics contributed to it consisted only in more frequent exploitation of modulations and key-configurations that had still been rare with Mozart and Beethoven. In this domain also, it was the nationally oriented non-German composers of the late Romantic period, like Dvořák and Smetana, Grieg and Niels Gade, Mussorgsky and Tchaikovsky, who introduced really "new" harmonic effects.

From the tonal-harmony–based simplicity of the early Classic onward, a steadily increasing refinement and exploitation of all possibilities in functional diatonic-chromatic-enharmonic harmony in the major-minor system is to be observed; it continued up to Debussy, Strauss, and Reger and in the late Romantic phase made more and more use of the stimuli offered by unlimited chromatic alteration and unlimited enharmonic interchange, broadening finally into polytonality but always remaining within the bounds of this tonal system. (A particularly characteristic case of polytonality that yet grew entirely out of the major-minor tonal system is to be found at the end of the third act of Strauss's *Rosenkavalier*.) For this reason the word "tonality" as used today for the most part tacitly implies this fully developed functional major-minor tonality, which now finds itself faced with "modality" on the one hand and on the other with the nonfunctional newer systems like the quarter-tone, the 19-step, the twelve-tone, etc. In its holding fast to this tonality the Classic-Romantic period shows itself, in contrast to its predecessors and its successors, to have been an indisputable historic entity.

How different the basic harmonic-tonal sense of the Classic era was from that of the preceding period is illustrated by its fundamentally different structural use of the keys. The late Baroque knew two different possibilities for the arrangement of the movements in a cyclical work and for the arrangement of the sections within the individual movements. The movements in such a work could either all be in the same key (in which case the tonic minor or major could replace the main key) as in the suite, or in variations, or especially in the chamber sonata; or they could pass by a sort of cadential formula through the closest neighboring keys (say: I–VI–IV–II–V–I or the like) as is the rule in, for example, Bach's church cantatas. Only the newer Italian categories like the instrumental concerto and the sonata da chiesa made numerous exceptions to this. In large cycles (acts of operas, sections of oratorios) usually no unified structural scheme dominates, perhaps not even any plan; tonalities are introduced individually, according to their affective value (Bach's *St. Matthew Passion* and B minor Mass are not tonally unified; Hasse's *Arminio* provides no recognizable "planned key-architecture." [24]

In the Classic era, on the other hand, the structural value of tonalities in a series of movements shows up clearly from the start. In sonata-like compositions the slow movements regularly provide a functional contrast to the rest; now and again the trio of the minuet is set in a related key but often also merely in the tonic major or minor. Variation cycles still cling to unity of key up to early Beethoven, but then occasionally assume (perhaps from his Op. 34 of 1802 on) irregular tonal variety. While in the early Classic era, key relationships between movements still generally adhere to the most closely related, in late Haydn there are already astonishing contrasts (for example, in the string quartets—in Op. 76, No. 5: D–f♯–d–D; in Op. 76, No. 6: E♭–b–B–E♭; in Op. 77, No. 1: G–E♭–G; in Op. 77, No. 2: F–D♭–D–F; in the Piano Sonata, Hoboken XVI, 52: E♭–E–E♭). In Beethoven similarly far-reaching contrasts occur; Mozart is more restrained in the tonal ordering of his movements and until well into his late period still holds to close key-relationships. Clementi sets all the movements of his famous B minor Sonata, Op. 40, No. 2, in the same key; Dussek, in choosing the keys for his Sonata in E♭, Op. 44 ("The Farewell"), obviously saw Beethoven's example hovering before his mind's eye. In Schubert, especially in his late works, it becomes

24. Rudolf Gerber, in *Das Erbe deutscher Musik*, XXVII, Leipzig, 1957.

clear how the play of color in the co-ordination of keys in the cycle replaces the structural value of tonality (String Quintet in C, D. 956, the so-called Op. 163—I: C; II: E-f-E; III: C-b♭ closing with b-C; IV: C). Whether tonalities are closely or distantly related, common to the composers of the Classic-Romantic period is their search to enliven and tighten the relationship between movements by use of key contrasts. The contrast binds the movements to one another, the tightenings strengthen the feeling of unity. Key contrasts between movements at times recur within a movement (e.g. Haydn Quartet Op. 77, No. 1, second to the third movement) and through the listener's memory contribute to the sense of connection.

A similar grouping or contrasting of tonalities characterized the Classic-Romantic style within the single movement. In the late Baroque it had been unity of key within the movement that counted; modulations and passages introducing neighboring keys emphasized rather than weakened it. In the early Classic period this situation changes in connection with the melodic-thematic structure. The late Baroque movement rests on the basic unity of the theme, and this is not canceled but fortified by contrapuntally introduced secondary themes or by contrasting episodes such as are the rule in, for example, the instrumental concerto. The early Classic style begins at once to dissolve this thematic unity in a colorful variety or at least in a plurality of themes. As early on as Domenico Scarlatti and Platti, and increasingly with Sammartini and Pergolesi, there appear in the Classic movement several melodic entities, independent of or even contrasting with each other, that have a more or less "thematic" character. They are apt to be introduced in tonal "planes" that are different from but for the most part closely related to the main key. The various planes of melodic happenings within the movement carry their own specific properties: rhythmic, harmonic, dynamic, and later, too, coloristic (and not only in music for orchestra). As distinct from the Baroque "style d'une teneur," the characteristic Classic-Romantic style brings together in a single movement the contrasts in the different spheres of expression, symbolizing them in contrasting tonal complexes. The energetic effect of the Classic-Romantic movement rests to no inconsiderable degree upon the contrast of such tonal planes and the final balancing out of opposites, and the tension aroused in the listener in large part depends on the extent of the tension in the tonal texture. Highly differentiated rhythms over a basically regular periodic structure that moves through areas of contrasting tonality: it is this that is distinctive for the whole style of the time.

In the early Classic phase, there is as yet no question of a regular application, even of any normalizing, of these key-relationships within the movement. Only in the High Classic period are they used in a manner that is to some extent regularized, as for instance the I–V (in minor, I–III) relation between the two main themes of the sonata movement; yet this I–V (or I–III) grouping can also, as often in Haydn, appear without any new melodic theme, so that two planes of tonality are used for the treating of a single theme, whereby the effect of a second theme is achieved. Similar contrasts in tonality are usual in rondo movements and are met with as early as Philipp Emanuel Bach. According to the rule, the theme appears four times in the tonic; in between, the first and third episodes are set in the same or a related key and the central episode likewise in a closely related or a more or less contrasting key (Johann Christian Bach's Piano-duet Sonata in C; [25] Beethoven's Piano Sonata in C minor, Op. 13; and, for divergencies, his Piano Sonata in Eb, Op. 7). It is not the rule that is important but the originality of the way in which changes in key and theme are linked with contrasts in motion and expression. Slow movements of symphonies, concertos, string quartets, sonatas, etc., often show such layers of tonality (for example, Mozart's Piano Concerto in C minor, K. 491, the slow movement: Eb–c–Eb–Ab–Eb, in which the tonally divergent episodes are also thematically independent and, being for wind-instrument groups, stand out from the string groups in the main key). Beethoven in his late works fully exploited the rich possibilities of such key contrasts within the movement (e.g. the Allegro assai vivace of the String Quartet in F

25. *Nagel's Musik-Archiv,* No. 4, Hannover, 1927, 1938.

minor, Op. 95; the Adagio of the String Quartet in E♭, Op. 127).
Here, it is true, the structural value of key changes begins to co-
alesce with color values: in late Beethoven contrasts in sound-
planes do not always serve that linking of constructive with expressive purposes which one finds in Haydn, Mozart, and Beethoven's
own earlier works; instead, tonalities change to meet the need for
intensified color that brings with it intensified expression, without
setting off structural components against each other. This was
picked up by the late Romantics (in the line from Wagner to
Strauss) who by predilection sought less a constructional than a
coloristic effect in the variegated play of keys; whereas the early
Romantics (Schubert, Weber, and the minor masters) apparently
much preferred to cling to the structural use of key changes, which
at the same time, indeed, provided highly intensified expression.

With this free use of tonalities in the cycle of movements and
within the movement, the Classic-Romantic era again stands in
contrast to all earlier periods as an historic stylistic entity. Great as
may be the distance from Stamitz to Bruckner in this regard, fundamentally the same feeling for tonality lives in both, and the way
in which they handle these elements is, as compared with all earlier historical periods, fundamentally the same. And with this the
Classic age stands as sharply in contrast to the Baroque as it does
to recent times, which seem to have lost the feeling for tonality
and harmony in the Classic sense.

c] Motif, Theme, and Thematic Development

Whatever the importance and the independence of
meter and rhythm, of harmony and tonality characterizing the
Classic-Romantic work of art, and however dense the integration
of these elements may be, Classic-Romantic music lives by melody,
its subtlest and most vital component. In the composer's "inspiration" these elements are integrated from the very start (he does
not invent a melody that he afterward equips with rhythm and harmony) but it is in the melody that the finest expressive value and
highest originality lie. The epoch is distinguished from its predecessors, in this even more than in elements of a metrical and

rhythmic, harmonic and tonal nature: never in the history of many-voiced music has melody played such a dominating role, and never has originality of melodic invention been regarded to such a degree as the stamp of value. The line of testimony to the art of melodic invention runs from Nichelmann to Richard Strauss. Periodicity, harmony, and the ordering of tonalities may be the building blocks of the Classic mansion of music; it is melody that lends it form, character, countenance. Melody is the soul of Classic music.

The basic differences between Classic-Romantic and earlier melody are self-evident. All older melody makes use either of a *cantus prius factus,* whether of chorale-like or songlike nature, or of certain formulas, *figurae,* more or less conventional in character, that were universally used and handed down from time immemorial in teaching the craft of composition. Keyboard music of the 17th century still rests in the main upon it. Perhaps nothing distinguishes a Froberger clavier toccata so fundamentally from a Mozart piano fantasy as the conventional constraint of melodic invention in the one, the inspired freedom in the other. Of course there are numerous transitional stages in between; nor did freedom of melodic invention fall like manna from Heaven upon the composers of the Classic period: it was worked for, and gradually attained. The era of J. S. Bach is such an intermediate stage. Italian opera had prepared the way for melodic independence, and although the voice parts of Hasse or Graun, even of Pergolesi or Jommelli may still be much constrained by the typical, there stirs in them the intent to give melodic invention an individual stamp. Bach and Handel were themselves sublime inventors of melody and for this reason, among others, appealed so strongly to the Romantic age; compared with them, composers like Telemann, Johann David Heinichen, *et al.* are left far behind in this respect. Just how the development toward Classic melody proceeded in detail has yet to be investigated. Certain it is that on the one hand Italian opera melody, on the other the desire for simplicity and the influence of folk music were involved in the process. At the same time that the so-called "Second Berlin Song School" was impressively representing the relationship with folk music, J. A. Hiller in Leipzig was defending Italian aria melody as a model of beauty. The contradiction is only an apparent one: in the background is evident the effort to achieve an individually expressive, characteristic, original, and at the same time easily accessible universal melodic language, in the fulfillment of which composer and listener co-operate.

An often stereotyped language is still characteristic of early Classic melody; the same turns recur frequently in different composers. Only after a long time does it become individualized. Wilhelm Friedemann and Philipp Emanuel Bach are among the exceptions; their markedly astringent and serious, often gloomy and irritably excited melodies stand out against the trivial tunes of Italian or South German composers. Expressive character in the sense of something unique, springing from a momentary mood, seems much more individual and original here than for instance among the Austrian composers or even the so-called "Mannheimers," whose melody, after a start at originality, quickly sank back into the conventional and who with their "manneristic Mannheimer taste," as Leopold Mozart called it, by no means found friends everywhere. Certain aftereffects of the doctrine of rhetorical figures are probably to be seen in Philipp Emanuel Bach's "principle of discourse" (*redende Prinzip*) and the "tons parlants" of French writers,[26] but the impression predominates of an instantaneously born, sensitive, overflowing, and often very personal melodic invention.

Typical of melody in the early Classic era—especially of instrumental melody, but of vocal melody as well, insofar as it is not of the Italian type (e.g. J. F. Gräfe's *Oden,* 1737; Telemann's *Lieder,* 1733, 1741; and further J. V. Görner, 1742, and C. G. Krause, from 1753 on)—are the brevity of its segments and the shortness of its breath. Instead of thinking in terms of the long-drawn breath of Italian opera melody, the intention here is to fol-

26. Arnold Schering, *Carl Philipp Emanuel Bach und das "redende Prinzip" in der Musik,* in *Jahrbuch des Musikbibliothek Peters,* XLV (1938). (Also in *Vom musikalischen Kunstwerk,* Leipzig, 1949, p. 213 ff.)

low faithfully the metric layout of the eight-measure period, which
causes the melodies to crumble into very small sections and lack
any undivided impetus. What is characteristic of them is not that
they are purposely constructed in this way but that they wear
themselves out in small-jointed articulation. The *galant* theme is
often limited to this tiny garden-plot idyll. Telemann's *Method-
ische Sonaten* (1728 and later; NA [27] I) still draw on the late Baroque heritage; his *Fantasien* for solo flute (c. 1730) and for solo
violin (1735; NA VI) form an odd mixture of old and new melody, probably owing to their unaccompanied monody, and represent perhaps the most vigorous side of his gift for melodic invention. This is also the case in his Duo Sonatas without basso
continuo, Op. 2 (1727; NA VIII), while his Six Sonatas for two
transverse flutes (NA VII, 2nd Series) already show all the marks
of the early Classic *style galant*. Telemann's *Harmonischer Gottes-
dienst* (1725–26; NA II–V) reveals similar transitional stages.
Quantz is a particularly characteristic representative of this sort of
melody. In Hiller's *Singspiele* of the 1760s small-jointed *galanterie,*
idyllic imitation of folksong, and Italian aria alternate. This same
small-jointedness is striking in Wagenseil, Franz Asplmayr, and
G. M. Monn; with the Bohemians around Stamitz it is often only
superficially hidden by the stormy sweep of invention. Far into
Haydn's and even in Mozart's early works this *galant* melody dominates the field; but it is to be observed that in the "sensibility"
phase (in Anton Filtz, for example, Ernst Eichner, Franz Beck,
Johann Christian Bach, Boccherini, but especially in Schobert,
J. G. Eckardt, J. F. Edelmann, *et al.,* and, for the vocal area, in
Anton Schweitzer and Ignaz Holzbauer, for example) the short-
breathed manner is overcome and gives way to songlike rather
than aria-like melody on a grander scale and with considerably
more expressive content. For vocal music one may perhaps assume
(most summarily) that a blend of small-scale *galant* melody, idyllic folklike song, and Italianizing aria quality came about along a
line running from Florian Leopold Gassmann through Georg

27. I.e. Georg Philipp Telemann, *Musikalische Werke,* Kassel,
1950– .

Benda, Johann Christoph Friedrich Bach, and J. A. P. Schulz to Christian Gottlob Neefe. In the German lied at any rate, the high point of the intermediate melodic stage appears with the works of Schulz, Johann Friedrich Reichardt, Carl Friedrich Zelter, and Johann Rudolf Zumsteeg. The new sort of expressive and individual melody that appears in these composers shows, simultaneously with Haydn's and Mozart's works of around 1770–80, the High Classic stage in the history of melody.

Meanwhile *galant* melody in the instrumental realm fell victim to the "singing allegro" of the Italians and Johann Christian Bach as well as to the *cantabile* manner of the slow movements of all the composers. Melodic style as such was no longer a problem in instrumental music of around 1770; the problem became one of melodic construction. The more invention aimed at individuality and expressive power, the more original it sought to be, the more it depended on the most characteristic possible stamp of the smallest unit, the "motif." It is in this respect that the Classic era parts most decisively with the late Baroque: there the motif is a common possession, now it is individual in the extreme; there it is essentially unalterable, now it is a germ capable of development, containing *in nuce* the expressive content of a movement. Within the frame of the structural period several characteristic motifs gather to form a "theme." The formative force must be strong enough to weld together the independent and self-willed forces of the motif in an energy-laden unity; only such a "whole" can act as a theme. More highly refined rhythm, more mobile harmony and tonality, often combined with color and dynamics give the composers of the High Classic a ready tool for establishing such a union of varied and divergent elements. The Classic is the first age to have known a "theme" in this sense. One can dissect Baroque "themes" into motifs, but their synthesis does not yield the tension-rich wholeness of variety and contrast in the structural period's unity achieved in the Classic era. In this process, too, there are of course transitional stages.

Corresponding with the metrical period and its subdivisions, eight-measure melodic structures—in two groups of four or four of

two, eight single measures, or alternating or varied groupings—
constitute the norm (of course extremely variable, never dealt with
schematically). The smallest melodic units, which are at the same
time rhythmic units—the motifs, that is—can be put together or
contrasted in all sorts of ways. (An example of alignment without
important harmonic, rhythmic, dynamic, or coloristic contrasts
would be the theme of the first movement of Mozart's Piano Sonata in A major, K. 331, with the scheme:

$$a\ a\ a\ b = 4\ \text{mm.} + a\ a\ a\ b' = 4\ \text{mm.}$$

For a somewhat more complex construction with all the above-
named contrasts, the opening theme of the same composer's Violin
Sonata in E♭, K. 481, with the scheme:

$$1\ 1\ 4 = 6\ \text{mm.} + 1\ 1\ 4 = 6\ \text{mm.} + 1\ 1\ 1\ 1 = 4\ \text{mm.}$$
$$a\ a\ b a\ a\ b a\ a\ a\ a$$

This gives a 16-measure period consisting not of 2×8, but of
$(2 \times 6) + 4$ measures, the melodic content of which is limited to
only two basic motifs.)

The motif is the smallest independent unit of energy in the
Classic shaping of form; meter, rhythm, harmony, color, dynamics,
and articulation are integrated with it as superordinate elements.
The theme is a more or less balanced unity of such motifs combined into a period. A "closed" character often inheres in the Classic theme, as is the case with the two Mozart examples cited
above: the motifs complement each other in diastematic rise and
fall, in functional harmonic succession, in rhythm, dynamics, etc.,
in such a way that the period results in a closed section. Yet such
completeness is not an inevitable feature of the Classic theme.
Haydn has a great many themes that remain "open," i.e. the motifs do not add up in diastematic, harmonic, or other relationships
to the impression of a closed section and leave the feeling that continued development is needed (for example, the themes of the first
movements of the String Quartets in C minor, Op. 17, No. 4; C
major, Op. 20, No. 2; G minor, Op. 20, No. 3, with 7-measure periods; F minor, Op. 20, No. 5; etc.). Mozart inclines more to
themes that are indeed many-jointed and full of contrasts, but

closed. Beethoven makes use of all sorts of possibilities.

With all composers, sonata-movement themes are more complex than those of slow movements and rondos. The inner equilibrium often comes about through repetition and use of analogous formatives; motifs follow either directly upon one another or in balanced groups (as in the two Mozart examples given above), a process that simultaneously achieves a great economy in melodic material. Motifs, too, can be contrasted in the same way: a b b a, a b a c, and countless variations of this sort are possible, so that contrasts arise within very limited space, charging the theme with detectable inner tension. Through appropriate harmonization corresponding groups of motifs can be related as statement-answer (as had already been done, purely melodically, in the medieval *ouvert-clos* endings). The possible extent of variation is practically infinite, yet the principle is always maintained. As a rule the theme stays within the frame of a simple or an extended period (extension is again served by repetitive and by analogous forms) and is confined to a single unified melodic event with the other elementary processes integrated into it. The tendency in the Classic era was not toward bursting the bounds of the period, but toward broadening it and stretching it to the limit of what can still be understood as a homogeneous process.

This happens with Mozart in his late works (cf. the first themes in the String Quartet in F, K. 590, and String Quintets in C and Eb, K. 515 and 614), whereas Schubert, for instance, in his later works is already, in complete contrast, working with complex themes—that is, themes that consist of several thematic groups in which several periodic processes come together in a complicated structure involving several events (cf. the first themes in the String Quintet in C, D. 956, the String Quartet in G, D. 887, the B minor Symphony). Here the Romantic complex theme is already present in its full development, as Bruckner was to carry it further with such mastery; yet the complex theme did not become the rule in the Romantic. In his early and middle works Beethoven creates themes that are, for the most part, strictly periodic and homogeneous, often surprisingly simple in structure, but later he inclines toward aphoristically abbreviated theme-structures that at times consist of only one or two motifs and without any real thematic delimitation pour their energies directly into the movement (e.g. the first themes of the F minor String Quartet, Op. 95, and those of the Ninth Symphony). In no other composer does such perfect sovereignty dominate the building of themes as in Beethoven. Complex themes as handled by Schubert correspond far more to "Classic" proportion than does the elemental arbitrariness with which Beethoven impetuously announces and unfolds his ideas. But it is just this aphoristic quality in Beethoven's themes that found many followers in the later Romantic period, as, for example, Berlioz, Wagner, and in the "New German" line up to Richard Strauss.

It is an indispensable property of the Classic-Romantic theme that it has to be capable of the most manifold alterations. In a Baroque work, motif and theme essentially change neither their form nor their content. In a Classic work it is just this that is definitive: the single motif, as well as the theme constructed of motifs, must be so made that they can undergo the most extensive changes and still be recognizable. Herein lies the core of the whole principle of "thematic work." The motif must remain undisturbed in its essential characteristics when it is transposed into various keys, combined at will with others, given different color, articulation, rhythm, or when, the rhythm remaining the same, it gives rise to a different melody, is differently harmonized, when it is inverted, lengthened, shortened—and it must be suited to all such transmogrifications. The basic motif of the first movement of Beethoven's Fifth Symphony remains recognizable in all its stages and transmutations. It is so constituted that it seems to throw off all these reshapings spontaneously out of its inherent energy: it is the motif itself that "works," not the composer with it—a fundamental contrast to all Baroque technique.

The theme, too, must be alterable in all directions. In addition it must have the property of being breakable into its motivic elements so that these work in the movement as parts representing the whole and can everywhere imply the existence of the theme, even where it is in reality only represented by its fragments. The degree to which such splitting and reuniting is actually carried or striven for varies from work to work; but axiomatically this is the principle underlying the Classic way of working.

This principle is most extensively used in the sonata movement; from here it frequently enters and takes possession of the rondo-finale, which is infused with sonata-movement elements and hence also with thematic development; it can govern stretches of the slow movement and can, in addition, be transferred to various types of movement. In the sonata movement the thematic work need not be limited to the principal theme; secondary themes can also be drawn in. In fact, thematic development can be employed in every instrumental and even every vocal movement, of whatever type. The objective of all thematic development is to unfold the expressive content of the theme, to transmute its material, exhausting all its possibilities. This often happens with substance that is most concise; whole movements of Haydn and Beethoven live on a few slight motifs, while Mozart likes the scope of a greater melodic wealth. The piling up of melodic ideas of all sorts is a criterion of the early rather than the High Classic era's manner of constructing a movement; to this extent Mozart in his early instrumental works still stays relatively close to the early Classic style; in the main he first came to economical, exhaustive thematic work under Haydn's influence from, say, the D minor String Quartet, K. 173 (1773) on. The High Classic style is concerned with the *multum,* not the *multa*—the much, not the many. The task of thematic work in the Classic-Romantic era—a task ever freshly enticing, ever solved in some novel, original manner—is to extract all possible expressive transmutations from material small in quantity but capable of subdivision and development.

This is accomplished by spinning the thematic thread along, developing, combining. The working material is "spun along" as it draws after it expressively altered, similar but substantially different configurations, summons forth contrasting themes, generates intermediary bridging elements, and thus unravels a chain of periods not alike in substance but logically connecting, of which one seems to "spin" itself unnoticeably out of another. The working material is "developed" when, the substance remaining the same, it is essentially altered, passing through every conceivable elemental dimension and in the process is filled with a constantly changing flow of expressive content, until it has yielded up all its inherent possibilities. The working material is "combined" as the available motifs become involved with one another, shifted about, handled in counterpoint or dialogue; as the positions of the themes in the movement are interchanged so that new, surprising combinations of materials in themselves familiar are arrived at (this last a preferred technique in Mozart's concertos); as (not infrequently in Haydn) new themes are introduced in counterpoint to those already present, or in a slow movement perhaps a songful theme calls forth a countersong to carry on a dialogue (very frequent in Schubert). Needless to say, the distinction between "spinning along," "developing," and "combining" is a theoretical attempt to keep apart categories of thematic work that in practice overlap in many ways and merge in innumerable nuances.

Basic to every possible sort of thematic work is the requirement, newly emerging in the Classic age, to continuously alter the expression of the music, to keep remodeling it in vital transitions and contrasts, regardless of whether the substance of the thematic work remains the same or changes. The music of the Baroque imitated types of emotion; the music of the Classic era mirrors the human psyche in its ever-changing moods. Modification of the substance is nothing but the form the composer finds for the flow of psychic impulses, for emotion and passion, for reverie and amusement, for exaltation and gloom, for strength of will and depth of suffering. To this extent thematic invention and development become the mirror of the composer's own soul. For the first time in music history the personality of the creative artist speaks of its own inner self, not in the sense of depicting some chance happening but in the sense that his own personal way of experiencing the world creates for itself a symbol of expression.

This takes place in a language for which there are no words but which, since it is a universal language, can be understood by everyone as long as it really remains so. The artist has now become the protagonist who gives form to human experience out of his own experience. This is "Classic" so long as he speaks the universal tongue, lifts experience into the sphere of the universally human, and allows the listener full freedom to co-operate. The Romantics, even from Wackenroder and Novalis on, elevated the artist to the rank of visionary, prophet, priest, and made him the mouthpiece of the divine. Thus comes to be expressed the recognition that there are creative musicians who, by their works, irresistibly draw the listener under their spell, proclaim the superhuman, and so raise music up into a temple of the higher life, removed from the mortal sphere. If, in addition, intensified means of expression are employed that compel the hearer to bow to the tyranny of this artistic intent and its enunciation, his free co-operation gives way to humble worship and instead of a purely and fully human music we have a music that seeks to be a religion, creating a distance between its own godlike solitude and the pitiful ordinariness of man—at this point, the frontier to the "Romantic" has been crossed. However that may be, this thematic invention and development, which forms the kernel of all composition in the Classic-Romantic age, is a most personal expression, such as no previous time had known, of the artist and his inner world in a work of art; as Hanslick put it, "composing is a working of the spirit in material that can itself become spirit."

d] Genres and Forms

Whereas the start of the Baroque was marked by the emergence of Italian monody, opera, the organ chorale, and so forth, new categories and forms appear scarcely or not at all at the beginning of the Classic era. Some older types die out, most rapidly perhaps the orchestral overture on the French model (which survived until late in the second half of the 18th century only in England), as well as the suite and the chamber sonata for various instruments, which may be regarded as extinct by around 1740. Innovations in the dance repertory result from current dance practice: allemands, courants, sarabands, gigues, rigaudons, loures, and

the like go out of fashion in both social and stage dancing; ga-
vottes, polonaises, minuets, long adopted in the Baroque, remain in
use and in part undergo gradual changes. The Classic era in its beginnings clearly tends to exclude the dance totally or almost totally
from higher art music: Wilhelm Friedemann and Philipp Emanuel
Bach banned it from their sonatas, and among the remaining composers only the minuet was left in the artistic sphere, being now
regularly equipped with a trio in place of the Baroque "Menuetto
II" (the name "trio" stems from the favored French scoring for
such episodes, in overture and ballet preferably consisting of two
oboes and a bassoon, and in the Classic era this term was simply
transferred to the intermediate section inserted before repetition of
the minuet proper). The minuet itself is modified either in the
direction of popular dance-types [28] or into the scherzo (originally
to be taken as "joking," later, especially by Beethoven, used more
and more as the name for an extremely agitated and tempestuous
movement supplanting the minuet), which has already found its
fixed place in Haydn's quartets designated as Op. 33 (composed in
1778–81). This does not exclude the composition of social dances
(widely pursued by most composers); but they remain social
dances, and only in the Romantic era does a new stylization begin
(Beethoven, Schubert, Weber, *et al.*), which then freshly introduces more recent dances like the ländler, waltz, écossaise, etc.,
into art music. The minuet may also, however, alter in the direction of a characteristic lyric piece, and behind titles like impromptu, eclogue, nocturne, moment musical, etc. (Schubert, Ja-
roslav Tomášek, Jan Hugo Voříšek, John Field, and so on), the
old familiar outline of the minuet still remains visible. Haydn and
Mozart, moreover, in their symphonies, string quartets, etc., often
raised the minuet to a highly refined chamber-music composition
sui generis.

Among instrumental categories the Baroque variation-cycle
continued to survive. Variations for piano particularly remained a
favorite subject throughout the Classic-Romantic period, at first
more in entertainment music for bourgeois and court circles, later

28. Cf. Ch. IV above.

more in the virtuoso concert. The principle, too, was directly taken over from the Baroque: unity of key with occasional use of the tonic minor or major, stereotyped metric and harmonic structure, ornamental figuration in treatment of the melodic voice; but the Baroque ostinato variation disappeared. The old features of an improvisational art thus survived in the variation cycle, and in fact all the Classic masters still frequently showed their skill in improvising variations at the piano. It is not such a long way from Froberger's *Mayerin* variations to Mozart's variations on *Lison dormait*. Unique achievements like Bach's *Goldberg Variations* found no imitators (a fact that even surprised Forkel in 1802); it was Beethoven, with his character variations, who first started on the road to freer handling of the piano variation, and the Romantics (Schumann and Brahms, for example) who first deliberately and unequivocally linked up with Bach's unique late work.

But along with these the development of the variation also followed other paths and above all in the introduction of the variation cycle as a movement in a large cyclic work. In the symphonies, sonatas, trios, string quartets, etc., of Haydn, Mozart, and Beethoven, the variation movement frequently occurs as a favorite component. Here the old improvisational model was surpassed in genuine further development and refinement, as for example in Mozart's Piano Trio in G, K. 564, in Haydn's *Emperor* variations in the String Quartet in C, Op. 76, No. 3, in those celestial variations in Mozart's A major String Quartet, K. 464, and finally in Beethoven's two sets of *Eroica* variations: the finale of the Third Symphony and the Op. 35 set for piano. Variations of this nature have in common not only preservation of the frame of the figurative variation above an unvarying metric-harmonic structure, but also characteristic alteration of the theme, giving it a totally different expressive value (cf. especially Mozart, K. 464), in this way achieving a sort of "thematic development" in variation form. In addition, the variation (even from Beethoven, Weber, and Schubert on) became more and more of a brilliant virtuoso showpiece. Beethoven's late variations (in Opp. 109, 110, 111; the Variations in C minor of 1806; the *Diabelli Variations*, Op. 120) combine in

a supremely authoritative manner features of the character variation with increased virtuoso demands.

The Baroque trio-sonata also continued to survive everywhere
at least into the early Classic period, among the Italian composers
as among the English (Thomas Arne, William Boyce, Humble),
the Germans, and the French. By the Italians, but particularly by
the North German school from J. J. Quantz to Graun and Philipp
Emanuel Bach, it was still much cultivated: in the latter school it
even gave rise to a special form with the order of movements
slow-slow-fast. Frenchmen like Leclair, Guillemain, Jacques Au-
bert, even François Joseph Gossec too, clung to the trio- (or indeed the quadro-) sonata, whose order of movements and melodic
and harmonic forms were gradually translated into the Classic
style. Around 1770–80, however, the old type was replaced by the
piano sonata with optional instruments (violin, flute), and out of
this then came the newer sonata for piano and obligatory instrument. The trio-sonata does not belong among the direct ancestors
of the Classic violin sonata; rather, the latter grew out of the new
piano sonata with an accompanying melodic instrument.

In a similar manner the Baroque concerto grosso was carried
on for a while in the early Classic period. Handel's Op. 6 (1739),
Francesco Geminiani's concerti grossi (which run at least to
1746), Charles Avison's concerti grossi (even to 1766) still retain
Baroque technique and form but are already latecomers for their
type. "England is one of the few countries in which the genuine
concerto grosso survived the invasion of the Mannheim symphony;
long after 1760 composers in England were still writing concerti
grossi of the Baroque type as well as *galant* sinfonie
concertanti." [29] Generally speaking, this category may be regarded
as having died out on the Continent around 1750. Whether it is to
be considered the direct forerunner of the Classic sinfonia concertante or whether the latter emerged rather from the new orchestral
symphony through the custom of introducing solo parts for various
instruments has not yet been made thoroughly clear. In any case,
those works of Holzbauer that belong in this category (*c.* 1760)

29. Charles Cudworth in MGG, article *England,* section E.

and Haydn's symphonies, *Le Matin, Le Midi, Le Soir,* (Hoboken I, 6–8; 1761) have nothing more of the old concerto grosso about them and are genuine concertante symphonies. This latter category, especially profusely cultivated by the Parisian composers around Jean-Baptiste Bréval, G. G. Cambini, St.-Georges, and others, by the younger Mannheim composers, and by Johann Christian Bach, came to full bloom in Mozart's concertos for two or more instruments (K. 297b [4 winds], K. 299 [flute and harp], K. 364 [violin and viola], and fragments) and his serenades; however, it later made only sporadic appearances (Beethoven, Op. 56 [piano, violin, cello]; Ludwig Spohr, Op. 48 [2 violins], Op. 88 [2 violins], Op. 131 [string quartet]; Schumann, Op. 86 [4 horns]; Brahms, Op. 102 [violin and cello]).

The solo concerto, on the other hand, was taken over without a break into the Classic age and further developed in the Classic style. The concerto for violin (less often for some other melody instrument) from Vivaldi, Alessandro Marcello, Francesco Veracini, Carlo Tessarini, Pietro Locatelli, and Giuseppe Tartini on, passed directly into the violin concerto of the Mannheim and North and South German masters as well as the French. Leclair, Simon Le Duc, and Pierre Gaviniès contributed to its further stylistic and violinistic development quite as much as Gaetano Pugnani, Antonio Lolli, G. M. Giornovicchi, and Giovanni Viotti, or in Germany Ernst Eichner, Carlo Giuseppe Toëschi, Franz Benda, Karl Stamitz, Ignaz Fränzl, Christian Cannabich, Johann Friedrich Eck, and many others. After J. S. Bach had raised the harpsichord to a concertizing instrument the production of keyboard concertos, too, kept right on. Willhelm Friedemann, Carl Philipp Emanuel, Johann Christian Bach, Graun, Johan Joachim Agrell, Georg Benda, Ernst Wilhelm Wolf, Carl Friedrich Abel, and countless other masters busied themselves with the writing of quantities of concertos. After Handel and Avison, the organ concerto continued to be cultivated in England (Arne, John Stanley, Thomas Dupuis, William Felton, Philip Hayes, James Hook, the Wesleys, William Crotch, *et al.*) [30] though no longer on the Continent.

30. *Ibid.*

In the Viennese school the keyboard concerto, after not particularly characteristic beginnings with Wagenseil, Leopold Hoffmann, Franz Dussek, and Joseph Haydn, quickly rose to the height of its development in Mozart. His piano concertos, far superior to those of all other composers of his time and also to his own violin concertos, belong to the crowning achievements of Viennese Classic instrumental music; a whole line of contemporary or younger composers followed him—Karl Ditters von Dittersdorf, Johann Baptist Wanhal, Leopold Anton Koželuch, the younger Dussek, Boccherini, Adalbert Gyrowetz, and others—none of whom managed to even approach his concertos. With Beethoven the piano concerto came to a certain terminal point for the Classic period; and his compositions in this form, too, frequently provided models for the Romantic composers. The three-movement ground plan remained unaltered from Baroque days; the principle of construction also remained unchanged. The first movement is begun and ended by two thematically rich ritornellos that also frequently appear whole or in fragments in the course of the movement, and between them, as a rule, the soloist is given three big solos while the orchestra is more or less busy with thematic work. In the Classic era, this ground plan is carried through with the symphony-movement's plurality of themes, so that in Mozart as many as five themes occur in the first movement of the concerto; not infrequently the soloist enters with his own themes, which may then be taken over by the orchestra, ample opportunity resulting for combinatorial work. The slow movement, often with reduced orchestral scoring, is treated in simple or extended song-form; here Mozart frequently unfolds the most enchanting complexity of sounds from the ensemble of piano, strings, and winds. The finale is constructed as a more or less free rondo movement, which can also include variation or sonata-like features. Both the instrumental scoring and the individual forms of the piano concerto long followed the Baroque model; it was not until Mozart that a greater use of winds became customary and symphonic forms penetrated the concerto. Then the concerto frequently (as in Mozart's and Beethoven's piano concertos) became very nearly a symphony with a concertizing solo instrument, and this it largely remained in the Romantic period.

The basic Classic form in general became the sonata movement, always combined with other movements to form a cycle: in the sonata, mostly with a slow, songlike movement and a rondo or variation finale; in the symphony, with a minuet or scherzo as well. The three-movement form remained fixed from the time of Alessandro Scarlatti's sinfonias and the keyboard sonatas of Platti, Sammartini, Galuppi, *et al.;* the four-movement form was taken up by the Mannheim group after Johann Stamitz and by the Viennese group after Wagenseil, Georg Matthias Monn, Matthaeus Schlöger, Josef Starzer, and the rest, while the Italians and the North Germans still adhered for a long time to the three-movement layout. The two-movement form occurs not infrequently with Italian composers, but also in Mozart's violin sonatas, in Haydn, and elsewhere; and if one wishes to regard Domenico Scarlatti's *Esercizi* as sonatas, one has come down to a single-movement form. Only in Beethoven's time did the four-movement cycle become the norm for both piano sonata and sonata for piano with some other instrument. In the symphony the four-movement form quickly won its way with the Germans (except for the North German school); the difference between the Italian and the German norm is shown by some of Mozart's symphonies composed for use in Italy: they originally had three movements, to which he added a minuet for their performance at Salzburg (e.g. K. 73, lllb); furthermore, a number of Mozart symphonies from these years have come down to us with but three movements.

The string quartet, on the other hand—in accord with its origin in part from the Italian string sinfonia and in part from the Viennese divertimento—in its early stages has sometimes three, sometimes five movements. The Haydn sets known as Opp. 1 and 2 (*c.* 1755–60?) which are indeed still called "cassations" or "divertimenti," have two minuets, and only beginning with Op. 3 (1760–65?; the authenticity of this series is debatable) does the four-movement form become an almost unbroken rule. As a well-established special chamber-music category for four solo players, the string quartet grew but slowly out of the *sinfonia a quattro* (four parts, but more than one player to the part) of the Italians from Tartini, Sammartini, Franz Xaver Richter, and others, to Haydn, Boccherini, the two younger Stamitz, and others. In other categories like the piano trio, the succession of movements vacillated for a long time and only from Beethoven's day took on the four-movement norm.

If all these categories relate more or less closely to the late Baroque heritage, nevertheless the divertimento, cassation, and serenade came forward as really new genres in the Classic period. The titles themselves are of earlier origin, but with the early Viennese composers—like Monn, Starzer, Augustin Holler, Asplmayr, Joseph Dorsch, Wenzel Pichl—and the Mannheimers—like Holzbauer, Franz Beck, Richter, Stamitz, *et al.*—they first came to stand for a series of five and often more movements of various kinds, the repertory of which runs from the genuine march and the air and variations to the solo-concerto movement, the symphony movement, and the rondo. The tremendous quantity of entertainment music of this sort written by every conceivable composer in the second half of the 18th century has yet to be thoroughly investigated. These categories reached the heights of inspired and refined development with Mozart; then, around 1800, they rapidly declined and fell into disuse. Their significance in the origin and development of the Viennese style can probably not be overestimated: with their folk elements and frequently evident preference for winds (cassation and serenade are mainly to be understood as outdoor music), they obviously made important contributions to the melodic and rhythmic style and the color characteristics of Haydn and Mozart. They are set for anything from full orchestra to large wind ensembles (Mozart's Serenades for thirteen and for eight instruments, K. 361, 375, and 388) down to trios (Mozart's K. Anh. 229 and 229a = 439b; Haydn's baryton trios) and to piano solo (Wagenseil, Giuseppe Antonio Paganelli, Dittersdorf, *et al.*). Here a direct passage opened up in the instrumental field from folk music to art music, and a category came into being that in its highest manifestations speaks, in its own way, an independent and novel "universal language."

Sonata form itself—the form of the sonata movement, that is, in symphony, string quartet, piano sonata, or wherever—evolved slowly out of Baroque beginnings. It was not "invented" in Vienna, or in Berlin, Mannheim, Milan, or anywhere else. Its outline goes back to the Italian sinfonia and sonata as they had been developed by around 1720: the movement is laid down in three sections, one that sets up the theme (exposition), a middle section the nature and task of which vacillates very much at first, and a closing section (reprise or recapitulation) that takes up the exposition again, in full or abbreviated. In the early Classic sonata movement, repeat marks as a rule close on the one hand the exposition and on the other the middle section together with the reprise; this latter repetition is found for a long time in Haydn and Mozart and was only gradually given up.

What may be regarded from the start as the distinguishing feature of the sonata movement is the treatment of tonalities. In the exposition the tonality changes at least once (I–V, in minor I–III or to some other closely related key) and this not by way of a passing modulation, but so as to set a new thematic member, in emphatically contrasting tonality, against the segment just concluded. Multiple changes in key may also occur but are rare. The middle section begins in the closing tonality of the exposition, or sometimes in a contrasting key, and moves along through modulations to close, as a rule, in the dominant. The recapitulation unifies the tonalities of the exposition by restricting them to the tonic. This is the norm fixed in the early Classic period.

Although it is often regarded as fundamental, the use of two subjects in the Classic sonata movement never became a generally recognized rule before Beethoven. The first movements of Haydn's symphonies and string quartets are for the most part kept monothematic, and to the main theme there is added an epilogue-theme that closes both exposition and reprise, rather than a proper "secondary subject"—that is to say, a substantially new theme of equal value brought in to contrast with the main theme. Mozart in his early days, on the contrary, prefers multiple subjects; only later

does his exposition consist mostly of a main and a secondary subject, joined by an epilogue-theme and sometimes by an intermediary theme between the main and the secondary subject. Most composers connect themes and structural members of the movement
by transitional passages of the greatest variety; but it can happen
in Haydn that the main subject governs the movement unrestrict-
edly or almost so. Not until early Beethoven did the thematic layout of two main subjects and an epilogue-theme become the norm.
With the early Classic composers, on the contrary, the plan varies
considerably: in Francesco Bartolomea Conti, Veracini, Platti,
Pergolesi, Philipp Emanuel Bach's early sonatas, Stamitz, Monn,
and others, two themes occur occasionally, but not as the rule;
multiple themes occur just as frequently—indeed, concretely delimitable themes are often not established, but the movement consists of a gay or turbulent swarm of all possible thematic fragments, as is often the case with the Mannheim symphonists. The
two-theme organization grew but slowly out of all this.

The handling of the middle section was for a long time similarly uncertain. For the most part, one can hardly speak, in the
early Classic period, of a "development" section in the sense of
thematic work. Instead, the middle section wrestles with new melodic material (as is so often the case in early Mozart), with free
modulation and sequential constructions (as in Johann Schobert
and C. P. E. Bach), and the like. The father of thematic work in
the sense of logically evolved thematic material, and hence also of
development, is without doubt Joseph Haydn. In his string quartets, from his first up to Op. 33 (1778–81), the path can be
clearly followed; yet in Haydn the thematic development often begins right after the theme and spins out through the whole movement, so that the "development" no longer appears as a special
section developing the theme but simply as the high point of thematic work in the movement. In his symphonies Haydn's treatment
of the middle section varies: nevertheless from the 1770s on it also
led to persistent thematic work, to a development section, and so
to the perfection of the Classic sonata movement for orchestra. In
his piano sonatas, again, the technique frequently changes. Lesser

masters like Dittersdorf, Wanhal, and others also made much varying use of the middle section. Mozart did not arrive at a genuine development section in symphony, concerto, or string quartet until after intensive contact with Haydn, and then he often handled it in a harmonically and colorfully rich way of his own. It was again Beethoven who established the norm for use of the middle section as the area par excellence for development, though from his piano sonatas Op. 27 on, it is true, he himself frequently upset this norm again. From the time of Haydn's String Quartet in C minor, Op. 17, No. 4 (1771) and his middle-period symphonies, a coda was often, even if not regularly, added to the three-section sonata movement as a closing member, allowing the movement to whirl more or less thematically to its close. Other additions, like the slow introduction Haydn used so much in his late symphonies, remained exceptions in the Classic period and were not copiously used until the later Romantic era.

The Classic sonata movement built on this plan became the foundation of Classic and Romantic instrumental categories. The four- (less frequently three-) movement cycle with the sonata movement at its head has outlived both the Classic and Romantic periods and still today provides the framework of many compositions scored for all kinds of forces. In the Classic era, this cycle underlies the symphony, the string quartet, the sonata for piano solo or with other instruments, the piano trio, and in a limited sense also the concerto. The sonata movement is only rarely replaced as introductory movement by a series of variations or a movement free in form (as in several of Beethoven's piano sonatas). Cultivation of a closer cyclical connection between the movements (perhaps through thematic or key relationships, references to or quotations of previous material, or closer contextual links) is to be observed from Haydn's middle symphonies and string quartets on, but only gradually became more general. Even Mozart often replaced movements he had completed (or at least begun) by others; the cycle connection in a more exact sense becomes unambiguous only in his last works. A single idea running through the whole, as it palpably underlies Beethoven's symphonies from the Fifth on, for example, became common practice only with the start of the Romantic era and then later in that period often gave rise to aspirations *per aspera ad astra:* the sonata movement becomes a struggle between opposing ideas, expressed in contrasting motives and themes; the slow movement deepens the content into the tragic or elevates it into the hymnic; the scherzo breaks in with ghostly daemonic fantasy; and the finale, in the Classic era almost always a "happy ending" or at least an ending in a spirit of reconciliation, is given the quite new task of gathering together all that has gone before and raising it to a triumphal apotheosis. Beethoven's Fifth and Ninth Symphonies were the models for this; they were still exceptional cases. Then in the Romantic world this program was often used as ground plan.

After Haydn's string quartets of Op. 20 it is not unusual to find the reactivated fugue as a technique of intensification in the sonata movement or in the finale; up to Beethoven's late works this remained a frequently used means for condensing and concentrating both in the movements and in the entire cycle. It seldom appears in pure form, mostly (as in Beethoven's Piano Sonata in B♭, Op. 106) as "Fuga con alcune licenze" or (as in Mozart's String Quartet in G, K. 387 or his Symphony in C, K. 551) is amalgamated in all sorts of ways with sonata-movement elements. The fugue is interesting in this connection not as a strict, self-contained, multiple development of a persistent theme, but as a link in the chain of thematic developments—that is, simply as a case of combinatorial work of a special stamp. Hence it is that fully achieved fugues seldom if ever appear; instead for the most part only fugal expositions, fugatos, or individual fugal developments. Counterpoint, otherwise favored in thematic work as "filigree work" (alternating appearances of thematic configurations in the different voices) or as "dialogue," may also from now on—the timidity of the Baroque model having been overcome—be used as a stricter form of the customary thematic work.

If a cycle begins with a sonata movement the whole composition is often called in generalizing fashion a "sonata." This term, used since the 16th century for the most varied of purposes, became firmly entrenched from early Classic times on for the piano sonata, and the sonata for piano with instruments ad libitum or with one or even two instruments obbligato. Compositions with sonata-form first movements for larger groups of instruments are called, according to their scoring, string quartet, string quintet, wind quintet, piano quartet or quintet (with strings, winds, or the like). If the composition is for orchestra, it is called a symphony, the old Italian term sinfonia being given a new sense. It is with these cyclic instrumental categories that the music of the Classic era, and German music in particular, achieved world importance. The derivation of the orchestral symphony and the sonata from the various sources of Italian, South and North German, and Bohemian music (including the Bohemians in Mannheim) has already been discussed; it seems scarcely necessary to describe its further course here. In the instrumental field, the Viennese style and the achievements of the Viennese High Classic period culminate in these cyclical categories. And in this field they have remained the "classic" solutions of the new problems of expression and hence the enduring and convincing productions of the Classic masters (cf. Chapter I). Their names and their basic forms have survived far into the 20th century. Today, despite all the changes music has undergone, they still provide the norms of composition for many composers.

The connection of the Classic era with the late Baroque remained even closer in the vocal than in the instrumental field. It is a widely held but erroneous idea that the Classic era was "the age of instrumental music"; that, in reality, was the Romantic era. The absolute precedence of instrumental music over vocal music dates only from Beethoven. The music of all composers from the early Classic Italians up to Beethoven unquestionably shows a fairly even distribution between vocal and instrumental production; according to his talents and his professional situation, one composer wrote more instrumental music, another more vocal music, and frequently in one and the same man (Dittersdorf, for example) the priority changes with a change of professional situation. In Haydn's and Mozart's productivity the balance is still evenly main-

tained. The testimony of contemporaries, however, from Herder
and Chabanon to Goethe and Jean Paul, shows beyond a doubt
that nonmusicians but slowly accustomed themselves to the newly
won significance and autonomy of instrumental music and for a
long time still saw in vocal music a category more accessible to
them and esthetically more satisfying. It is indicative that with
Wackenroder, Tieck, Novalis, and E. T. A. Hoffmann, on the contrary, instrumental music suddenly moved to the forefront, it being
the kind of music that more readily allowed the composer to express himself, to step before a public as seer and priest, to waft the
listener into the high realm of his divine prophecying or the ecstacy of his daemonic power.

The church-music categories changed least of all. An unbroken
line leads from the concertante Mass of Caldara and J. J. Fux to
the two Reutters, Franz Tuma, the two Haydns, and Mozart, while
the new melody and rhythm, the new thematic use of instruments,
and the symphonic and other features of the Classic style found
their way but slowly into the Mass. Mozart's fragmentary Mass in
C minor (K. 427, 1782–83) is an example of the fusion of styles
that ensued or had been under way. Joseph Haydn's late Masses
(1796–1802) are, it is true, thoroughly "classic" in their stylistic
manner, but achieve this classicity without any break with the past.

Even compositional technique in these Masses remained conservative in its details: at certain points (e.g. *Christe, Benedictus*)
the solo movements favored by tradition appear; at others (e.g. the
close of the Gloria and the Credo) choral fugues; the orchestra is
busied throughout whole sections of a movement with consistent
figures and formulas to keep up motion and only seldom takes on
obbligato or genuinely symphonic tasks. In the background of this
persistence lies the fact that this church music is still felt to have a
liturgical function, or to be at least an ornament to divine service.
Only as it begins to free itself herefrom, and itself becomes a Romantic "religion of humanity"—as suggested in Beethoven's Mass
in C (Op. 86, 1807) and perfected in his *Missa solemnis* (Op.
123, 1819–23)—does it give up the old restrictions and techniques
in favor of the composer's own independent interpretation of the

Mass text, carried out by all the means available to the Classic style. It is indicative that Schubert's Masses and even Bruckner's early church works are much more "classical" than Beethoven's *Missa solemnis*.

With all the smaller church-music categories—vespers, litanies, and the like—things went much as with the Mass. Alongside concertante church music the *a cappella* polyphony of Palestrinian origin remained in use (to this extent the Baroque dichotomy of ancient and modern styles continues). It found a master in Michael Haydn, who translated its technique into the language and sound-world of Classicism and whose compositions remained in use all through the 19th century. In these areas, then, the Baroque heritage was smoothly transferred, with stylistic alterations, into the Classic and Romantic periods. On the Protestant side, Bach's pupils and successors—like Gottfried August Homilius, Johann Friedrich Doles, and many others—kept the tradition of the church cantata alive, a tradition which nevertheless levels off more and more into an epigonal classicism and despite all efforts on the part of church musicians, gradually succumbs by the turn of the century in consequence of the declining situation of church music. Here it was that the awakening Bach revival first led to a process of historicizing revitalization, while at the same time, due to the initiative of Carl von Winterfeld, historical interest in reviving the works of the old masters gained acceptance in evangelical church music.

Opera seria, too, was smoothly taken over from the late Baroque into the Classic period. It survived astonishingly long as court opera for festivals and ceremonial occasions; Mozart's *Titus* (1791) is a late example of how—the libretto (reworked from Metastasio) and the formal layout remaining the same—the musical style adapted itself completely to the Classic mode of expression. In Germany, the specifically German form of Baroque opera lasted until around 1730 in Hamburg, Braunschweig, and elsewhere. Then followed the invasion of the so-called "Neapolitan" opera with its peripatetic Italian opera troupes. Cultivation of opera in the cities remained irregular into the 1780s, and only at the courts did fairly regular opera theaters survive. In France, for serious opera the Lully type of tragédie lyrique together with stage ballet prevailed until Rameau. The early Classic spirit had already entered into the libretto of opera seria with Metastasio (from 1723, *Didone abbandonata*), in a certain sense even with Zeno (first texts around 1700). The bewildering diversity of Baroque action, scenery, language, and characteristics had been replaced by the sober strength of enlightened virtue and stoic heroism. Since the operas of Handel, Bononcini, Vinci, Leonardo Leo, Pergolesi, Hasse, Graun, and many more, a vast flood of "Neapolitan" opere serie up to Johann Christian Bach, Nicola Antonio Porpora, and others had swept across Europe, musically noteworthy for the virtuosity of their solo roles and the wealth of their brilliant coloratura. The group of so-called "Reform Neapolitans" around Jommelli, Tommaso Traetta, Giovanni Majo, *et al.* stands out from this flood. Among their followers, Gluck on the German side, but in a certain sense also Niccolò Piccinni, Antonio Sacchini, and others on the Italian side, then shaped a type of opera that henceforth both in content and music was outspokenly "Classic." The stage pathos of the past, grown stereotyped, was now felt to be "false"; "true" representation of universally human "empiric" characters appears as the high objective that concerns no longer only a society of classes but mankind itself. From here a straight road leads to Beethoven and Cherubini.

Alongside opera seria, with Gaetano Latilla, Francesco Provenzale, and Pergolesi, there had appeared the comic intermezzo and the opera buffa that grew out of it, types that with their popular realism and their keen rationality present themselves from the start as children of Classicism far rather than of the Baroque. The Italian buffa also had spread over most of Europe; it was responsible for unleashing the battle in France against the rigidity of tradition and for loosening the tongues of musicians and literati of all nations. An infinite quantity of such operas was performed all over Europe; at the end of the 18th century the genre was still enjoying triumphs with Cimarosa, Giuseppe Sarti, Giovanni Paisiello, and others. With Jean-Jacques Rousseau's *Le Devin du village*

(1752), the French musical play with spoken dialogue reached
Germany too (Gluck paid it homage with several works), and in
its wake the domestic musical comedy in the shape of opéra comique (which, in the same middle-class spirit that characterizes
the comedy, could then turn into the domestic tragedy) also had
conquered Europe's stages in the hands of Egidio Romoaldo Duni,
François André Philidor, Pierre Alexandre Monsigny, and Grétry.
Preceded by the English ballad opera and its French model, the
Singspiele of Johann Adam Hiller, Christian Gottlob Neefe, Ignaz
Umlauf, Johann André, and many others came to life, the blending of national styles having been accomplished in them just as
convincingly as in opéra comique. Out of all these trends there
finally came about—with *Alceste* and *Rosamunde* (1773 and
1777; collaborations of the poet Christoph Martin Wieland and
the composer Anton Schweitzer) and Holzbauer's *Günther von
Schwarzburg* (1777)—those efforts at creation of a serious national German opera that eventually did indeed produce, in *The
Magic Flute* and *Fidelio,* great masterpieces, though these offered
only partial solutions to the underlying problem. These efforts lead
directly to the Romantic opera of Weber and Spohr.

The history of opera in the Classic era offers a confusing picture of constantly crisscrossing currents and tendencies, in which
Baroque heritage long remained alive while Classic feeling early established itself, and all of which were eventually saturated with national elements and so mingled and mixed as to become indistin-
guishable. The intermediary and secondary categories that arose,
like the opera eroica-comica, the dramma giocoso, the mono- and
duo-drama, etc., complicate the picture beyond all measure. The
intermingling influences of several generations contributed to the
keeping alive of older models and styles where newer ones had long
been evolved, but it also frequently compelled composers to be
writing side by side in different styles. In 1771 Hasse, at seventy-
two, produced his last opera seria in Milan, where the fifteen-year-
old Mozart was competing with him in the same field. The relation
of individual composers to categories and tendencies varies from
case to case and is very often determined by the purposes for

which the work was commissioned. Haydn wrote Italian opere
serie (rather of the reform-Neapolitan type) and buffe that in the
main followed the Italian models; Mozart united the Singspiel
with seria, buffa, opéra comique, and dramma giocoso with a fore-
cast of German Romantic fairytale opera—and perhaps through
this very many-sidedness created operas that (along with those of
Gluck) reached far beyond the limits of the century.

The 18th century was the century par excellence of opera. The
number of operas composed and produced is still beyond all
estimation. Much research is still needed to uncover its history in
detail and trace it back to the basic Baroque, Classic, and Romantic currents controlling it. Next to church music it is the field of
musical composition in the Classic era richest in tradition, next to
the new instrumental music the most progressive, and nowhere
save in the lied did the esthetic of word-and-tone relationship bring
about such definitive new forms as in the opera. Certain it is, too,
that the predominating interest of the Classic era up to Beethoven
lay not in orchestral music, church music, chamber music, or lied,
but in the opera.

Like the opera, the oratorio also continued to be cultivated as
a heritage. In South Germany and in Italy the Metastasian type of
oratorio, represented by Hasse, Porpora, and almost all the opera
composers of the time, survived well into the 19th century. At the
same time Johann Ernst Eberlin appears with oratorios in an advanced Classic style. With these two trends correspond, say,
Haydn's *Ritorno di Tobia* (1774) and Mozart's little Italian oratorios. In North Germany, one oratorio tradition ended with J. S.
Bach, but from Telemann via Graun (*Der Tod Jesu,* 1755), Johann Ernst and Johann Christoph Friedrich Bach, to Johann Heinrich Rolle, a sentimental trend in oratorio, influenced by the Enlightenment, was further pursued, one that put forth a secular
branch alongside the spiritual one (with its so-called "Jesus oratorios"). According to Schering, some six or eight types of oratorio
existed simultaneously.

Empfindsamkeit—"sensibility"—offered fertile soil for this
genre. The contemporary English oratorio composers like Greene,

Boyce, Stanley, Arne, and Arnold sought rather to carry on with the biblical oratorio in the manner of Handel. Haydn's *Creation* and *Seasons* (1798 and 1801) linked Handelian impressions with English texts and elements of Singspiel, opera, even church music, symphony, and lied, and with the characteristics of his own mature style. They bear testimony to that starry hour of human history in which the unity of highest art with highest popular national quality was brought to realization by the creative powers of the composer then the most famous in the world. In the opinion of the *Allgemeine musikalische Zeitung,* [31] *The Creation* was "Kunstvolle Popularität oder populare Kunstfülle"—the popular raised to consummate art, or high art saturated with popular elements. With the unique exception of *The Magic Flute,* there are simply no other works of the time in which the universal language spoke in such degree to all mankind or was in such degree understood by all as in these two late oratorios of Haydn. Not without good reason have they retained their vitality until far into the 20th century. Beethoven's Ninth Symphony and the closing section of his *Fidelio* (both in a sense "oratorical" works) attempt something similar but were not able to achieve the totally pervasive effect created by Haydn, at least not until later generations.

The German lied, finally, is a distinctive product of the awakening and unfolding Classic spirit, one that has a very similarly directed parallel in the English song of Henry Carey, Boyce, Arne, Charles Dibdin, James Hook, and others. In this category the popular tendencies of the time were able to take their own characteristic form and unite with the highest kind of poetry. Telemann and Johann Valentin Görner had made a decisive start at an idyllic bourgeois or narrative solo song with basso continuo in simplest forms, which deliberately turned against the overrefined Baroque ornamentation and virtuosic Italian aria melody. With the two "Berlin Song Schools"—the "First" centering around the writer Karl Christian Friedrich Krause and the poet Karl Wilhelm Ramler (the two Grauns, C. P. E. Bach, Franz Benda, Quantz, Johann

31. Eberhard Preussner, *Die bürgerliche Musikkultur,* Hamburg, 1935. On p. 83, Preussner quotes from the *AmZ* of 1801.

Friedrich Agricola, Christoph Nichelmann), and the "Second" around J. A. P. Schulz—a new art song arose in the course of hardly more than thirty years, which in its open sincerity and its conformity without artifice to the poetic text embodies the very fundamentals of the "Classic." With its best masters—like Zelter, Johann Friedrich Reichardt, Neefe in North Germany, Johann Rudolf Zumsteeg, Christoph Rheineck, Daniel Schubart, and Hans Georg Nägeli in South Germany and Switzerland—the German song attained a height of classic validity that scarcely aroused comparable powers in Austria with men like Josef Anton Steffan, Johann Holzer, and others, but in the young Franz Schubert found its culmination and the transition into a more Romantic trend in which the music rose above the poetry by absorbing it and then continuing the creative process on its own terms. Here the songs of Haydn and Mozart stand only on the peripheries, and in this category Beethoven but rarely found the tone befitting the high quality of this intimate art. Though a successful and generally valid solution to the problem of a full-fledged German serious opera may not have been arrived at (or only in the one lucky case of *The Magic Flute*), yet the modest category of the song was able to meet in a fully adequate manner the demands and ideas of Classic poetry and the esthetic challenge of a universal language close to people. Reichardt, Zelter, Zumsteeg, and the rest were no "forerunners," they were fulfillers rather; but while in instrumental music the Classic repertory remained valid alongside the Romantic, in the song the Romantic trend was later to overshadow the Classic.

VI

The Orchestra and the Classic Concept of Sound

In terms of sound, the Classic age received its identifying characteristic from the orchestra, the "modern" orchestra that developed at this time. Yet the orchestra is but one of the media in which the new tonal requirements found expression; other instrumental ensembles, like the string quartet, quintet, and trio, the piano trio, and the sonata for piano with obbligato instruments, are just as typical. The fixed instrumental groups that took shape with classical music are of a new sort altogether, even if the instruments of which they made use were not. Since the close of the 17th century (Corelli) the violin had moved into first place among string instruments; in association with viola and violoncello, likewise members of the violin family, it had gradually replaced the older viol forms. The process came to an end in the pre-Classic phase. After the middle of the 18th century the viola da gamba appears as a solo instrument only sporadically (as in Karl Friedrich Abel and Tartini), and the same is true of the viola d'amore (as with Karl Stamitz); that their use did hang on is shown by the fact that one Louis-Toussaint Milandre could still publish a *Méthode facile pour la viole d'amour* in 1782. Odd forms like the baryton, for which Haydn composed so much, remained fashionable curiosities. The violin won a position of absolute sovereignty as a solo and orchestral instrument. From Giuseppe Jacchini (published in 1701), Evaristo dall'Abaco (1712–14), and Leonardo Leo (1737–38) up to Beethoven the violoncello was occasionally given solo passages and in addition had won for itself the next most important place to the violin's among the strings in orchestra and chamber-music ensembles, while the viola was and remained specifically an orchestral instrument.

The plucked instruments, too, managed to carry over from the late Baroque into the Classic age. The lute was still used for solos until about 1750 (Sylvius Leopold Weiss, Ernst Gottlieb Baron, Adam Falkenhagen, David Kellner, Karl Kohaut), but its long period of flourishing was over. As thorough-bass instruments, on the other hand, lute, harp, theorbo, and gamba survived to the end of the 18th century, on occasion even beyond. In the late 18th and early 19th centuries the harp was even a particularly favorite instrument of virtuoso and dilettante.

Among the woodwinds, the transverse flute was indispensable in the early Classic era as a solo, ensemble, and orchestral instrument (the recorder or beaked flute disappeared entirely around 1750). Its delicate, languishing, sweet tone changed more and more, to be sure, into the full, masculine, even piercing tone Quantz wished for. Its role in the 18th century as the instrument of amateurs can hardly be overestimated. But in the High Classic period its importance as a solo instrument diminished, though it retained its firm place in the orchestra. It is significant that in the early Classic phase it was ranked as a solo instrument with the violin and oboe and could be interchanged with them, but that Haydn, Mozart, and Beethoven used it only rarely outside the orchestra. Oboe and bassoon, the characteristic woodwinds for the late Baroque orchestra, kept their respective functions as leading melody and bass instrument in the orchestra and ensemble of the Classic period as well. As a solo instrument the oboe retreated more and more into the background, and for it, too, the masters of the High Classic era only rarely wrote solo compositions (the bassoon was only exceptionally used soloistically, for tone color in opera and the like). The clarinet, on the other hand, formerly used only occasionally, around 1750 came to be included in the woodwind orchestral group as an equal. From the 1740s on it is found in Paris, Mannheim, Frankfurt, from the 1760s on, in London and Milan; and by composers from Johann Stamitz and Johann

Melchior Molter to Mozart it was also used, albeit fairly seldom, as a solo instrument. Its alto variety, the basset horn, was never taken into the orchestra as a permanent instrument, and was entrusted with significant tasks only by Mozart.

From the mid-18th century the French horn belonged in the orchestra as a fixture among the brasses, and here it quickly won a permanent place as an indispensable support of orchestral color. If flutes or oboes are occasionally missing in the classic orchestra, if even in Haydn's and Mozart's last works clarinets are fairly often missing, the horns are never absent. The horn, too, stems from the late Baroque heritage and is encountered in the works of the Hamburg opera composers, in Bach, in Handel, in Vivaldi, and at the court of Kremsier (now Kroměříž in North Moravia) [32]—but as an occasionally used solo instrument rather than as a regular member of the orchestra. In the Classic period it always remained rare as a solo instrument (Haydn, Mozart) but is plentifully found in divertimento, cassation, serenade, and dance music. Its rapid spread is probably to be traced to its use in the dance and serenade music of itinerant Bohemian musicians. The trumpet, characteristic for the late Baroque festival orchestra (where it occurs mostly in twos or threes, as a rule with kettledrums), was also taken into the Classic orchestra for its color effect; throughout the period (from Bach's Second Brandenburg Concerto to Haydn's Trumpet Concerto of 1796) it was only rarely used as a solo instrument.

During the whole period, the trombones were employed (mostly in threes) as reinforcement to the chorus in church music; only from Gluck's *Alceste,* Mozart's *Don Giovanni* and *Magic Flute,* and Beethoven's Fifth Symphony on were they given obbligato parts in the orchestra and used for their color. Other instruments, such as the piccolo, the double bassoon, etc., appear only sporadically in the Classic orchestra.

Although no single instrument in the Classic orchestra (except for the clarinet) is new, their relationships to each other and manner of use did change. The string body of the late Baroque orches-

32. E. H. Meyer in *Die Musikforschung,* IX (1956), 388 ff.

tra was five-voiced on the French pattern (two viola parts); with
the Italian sinfonia (hence already an early Classic element) it was
reduced to the four voices that have since then been its basis; not
until the late Romantic era did it move to a new kind of five-voice
group through the use of independent double bass parts. In the
late Baroque orchestra the woodwinds were always set in choirs
corresponding to the strength of the strings; this practice (predominantly in church music) is firmly retained well into the close of
the 18th century.[33] With the beginning of the early Classic period,
however, it became the rule to set all the wind instruments in pairs
(save for the flute, which is often single). Three and four horns
are the exception; not until Beethoven and Weber did the four-
horn pattern come into frequent use, and in the Romantic orchestra this practically became the rule. The total complements are
often astonishingly large: 24–30 violins, 10–20 other strings,
10–16 winds, kettledrums and thorough-bass instruments being no
rarity. Beethoven demanded an orchestral strength of up to 60 instruments, yet in Vienna in the *Tonkünstler-Sozietät* (Society of
Musicians), at Prince Hildburghausen's and elsewhere, music was
often made with orchestras of over a hundred persons. In Paris in
1828, François-Antoine Habeneck is supposed to have had at his
disposal some 60 strings beside doubled woodwinds and brasses.
However, such large numbers—and especially the doubling of
winds—must have been exceptional.

The thorough-bass was in many cases retained until the end of
the century; in church music and Italian opera it was widely regarded as indispensable until well into the 19th century. Yet the
effect of a harpsichord or even of an early fortepiano on the sound
of such orchestral forces could no longer have been of consequence; only in the opera, where the accompaniment to recitative
had to be improvised, did the thorough-bass instrument retain a
really necessary role. Haydn, it is true, still sat at the harpsichord in
performances of his symphonies in London, but the direction lay
in the hands of the concert master Salomon, and the composer's
keyboard accompaniment could only have been a formality. In

33. Robert Maria Haas, *Aufführungspraxis,* Potsdam, 1932, p. 218.

any case, the thorough-bass was generally given up in orchestral music around 1800.

The fascinating sound of the new symphony orchestra was due in part to the augmenting of the strings, in part to the new way of using the winds and exploiting their specific colors. In the late Baroque orchestra the winds either had soloistic tasks to perform or were treated in choirs—oboes and bassoons as a unit, trumpets and kettledrums as a unit, flutes more soloistically—and frequently they merely played in unison with the strings or with the voices. Even in the Baroque period composers had indeed set a value upon shaping their wind-instrument parts more and more "idiomatically," in accord with their technique and tone; their specific color, however, was seldom exploited in the process. Horns are distinguished from cellos, oboes from violins by their different playing techniques, by range, register, dynamic strength, but not basically by color; hence it is that in early Classic as in late Baroque music instruments can frequently be interchanged without in any way harming the work.

With the Mannheim symphony (in this aspect perhaps influenced by Rameau) the sense for color effect awoke (and more clearly here than with the Italian, the Viennese, or the North German composer groups); herein perhaps lies the really special contribution of the Bohemian musicians resident in Mannheim in comparison with others. In Philipp Emanuel Bach and in the early Haydn, color does not yet play a determining role; but with Haydn's middle-period symphonies (shortly before and after 1770), and in Mozart's early works of the same time, color stands out as a characteristic element, and soon its structural values, too, are recognized. The natural, naïve sound of horns and clarinets had from the start introduced a romanticizing element into the Classic orchestra. Mozart's ability to combine the specific color effects of the various strings and winds in ever new tone-colors, to develop them in new areas of expression, the irresistible sensuousness of his coloration and the unique degree to which he integrated color, tonality, harmony, melody, and rhythm lift him far above all lesser contemporaries, often above Haydn and Beethoven as well.

At this point in the practice of orchestral composition arose the
new art of instrumentation, which Beethoven himself took over as
a heritage, which then became, from Weber and Berlioz on, one of
the chief concerns of the Romantic composers, and which from
Valentin Roeser (1764) on led via Louis-Joseph Francoeur and
others to Berlioz and thus to the modern theory of instrumentation. Without doubt this—the giving form in living sound to what
is indeed inherent in the notes but must be extracted from them—
is one of the most fundamental innovations of all time, one of the
absolutely determining basic elements of Classic music, and one of
the causes of its universal validity.

The orchestra thus constituted has been enlarged and strengthened since the Classic period, enriched by a few instruments, but
basically not altered. The technique of orchestral playing, too, has
remained unchanged, founded as it is on strict discipline, uniform
bowing for the strings, precise articulation by all instruments, and
the merging of all into a perfectly homogeneous totality of sound
(in contrast to the cleavages in late Baroque sonority). Johann
Adolf Hasse and Johann Georg Pisendel in Dresden, Graun in
Berlin, Stamitz and Cannabich in Mannheim, Jommelli in Stuttgart, Haydn in Eisenstadt and Esterház, and many others were se-
vere trainers of their orchestras; the fruits of their labors have
nourished two centuries, and today's perfectionism is nothing but
the ultimate heightening of their technique. With an orchestra so
trained, too, the much-admired dynamic effects could be achieved;
the orchestras of Mannheim and Stuttgart were famous beyond all
others for their finely graduated playing, their fortissimo and pian-
issimo, their crescendo and diminuendo, their sforzati, etc. This
technique is to be observed earlier in Rome and Paris, but seems
now to have been consistently applied to the orchestra for the first
time and intensified to achieve the effects that so stirred countless
contemporaries from Schubart to Jean Paul.

It is perhaps significant that throughout the Classic period the
direction of this orchestra with its novel effects remained essentially unchanged from that of the Baroque; pure orchestral music
was led by the first violinist (concertmaster) with bow and ges-

ture, and vocal music with orchestra was led by the maestro at the harpsichord with his thorough-bass chords and body motions. So it remained from Bach's and Handel's time until the early years of the 19th century. Beethoven, Gottfried Weber, Anselm Weber, Gasparo Spontini, Carl Maria von Weber, and Spohr conducted with a little baton or a roll of paper or the like. Not until the start of the Romantic era did the conductor step forth from among his player-colleagues, become an interpreter, and impose his personal conceptions on orchestra and public.

The Classic blending of sound became standard for all other instruments and their development. By the middle of the 18th century the organ lost the choir-like segregation of its tonal colors and came ever closer to imitating the orchestra; its stops borrowed their tone quality and names from orchestral instruments, and its swell mechanisms provided a way of imitating the orchestra's dynamic effects as well. Among keyboard instruments the fortepiano rapidly took precedence from the same time on, at first still thin-sounding and delicately strung (J. A. Silbermann, J. G. Wagner, Stein, Walter, Érard), then developing quickly in strength and capacity for gradation until Shudi (Tschudi) and Broadwood built —still in Beethoven's lifetime—an orchestra-like piano that met all requirements in dynamics and articulation and that in principle has remained unaltered until today. Playing of the fortepiano spread slowly. Even in his old age Philipp Emanuel Bach still preferred the clavichord; in their early days Haydn and Mozart also used the clavichord or the harpsichord, the latter instrument also surviving as thorough-bass instrument until the end of figured-bass playing. One may assume that from about 1770 on (with marked differences in different countries, of course) the Classic klavier, i.e. the pianoforte, became the most important keyboard instrument: as solo instrument it rapidly won equal rank with the violin, and until now it has remained, with the violin, generally speaking the most important of all musical instruments. If the masters of the Haydn-Mozart period still obviously take into consideration the weak tone of the instrument and in their piano compositions aim at lucidity and chamber-music tone qualities rather than fullness and power,

Beethoven, even in his early piano sonatas, like his contemporaries Clementi and the younger Dussek, already achieved a pronouncedly orchestral texture. A Mozart piano sonata cannot be orchestrated, but in the 19th century Beethoven's piano sonatas were used as practice material in the teaching of instrumentation.

It is obvious that the Classic orchestra with its novel sound effects reflects the ideal sonority of the time itself. Man's requirements in sound had moved into a new age. The great epochs of music history are not only epochs of compositional techniques, of categories and forms, they are not only differentiated by changes in the area of basic elements; they are, perhaps above all, epochs in man's conception of musical sound and what he demands of it.

VII

The Public Concert and
the Role of the Musician

The musical phase of the Classic era coincides with the ripening of an emancipated middle class. The Classic period of music is at the same time its middle-class period. In the Baroque, music was carried on mainly at court and in church; princes, aristocrats, and cathedrals were its principal supporters. In Protestant circles church music and city (i.e. secular) music were widely concurrent; most of the leading church musicians were at the same time directors of music in the cities. Since the 17th century starts had indeed been made in various places at a concertlike public musical activity. The beginnings of the public concert lie, on the one hand, in the private organizations of individual amateurs in England and the public performances of church music that had become customary in Holland and North Germany; on the other, in performances at academies and conservatories in Italy which had long been attended by both aristocracy and bourgeoisie. Yet all these earlier concertlike undertakings still lacked the character of speculative enterprise that apparently first began to develop in the beginning of the 18th century.

The decisive step lies in the fact that the musician now goes before the public no longer by reason of his office but as an artist, himself responsible for and remunerated by his performance; that some civic association or some individual concert-manager (in the case of a virtuoso concert, frequently the artist himself) finances the undertaking; and that basically anyone can attend on payment of an entrance fee. Their regularity soon became a further characteristic of such events; concerts were often given on a subscription basis. This new form of impresario-concert did not occur suddenly but developed gradually out of the earlier concerts (called "academies"), church music, performances by *collegia musica,* etc., and appears to have been widespread from the beginning of the 18th century. According to Preussner,[34] public concerts of this type already existed in Strasbourg, Augsburg, Frankfurt, Bern, Lyons, Bologna, and Rome around 1710–20. In England a long series of concert undertakings took place after the founding of the Academy of Ancient Music in 1710.

The model for all such organizations all over Europe, and at the same time one of the most famous throughout the 18th century, was the Concert Spirituel in Paris (started in 1725), which was followed in France itself by a large number of similar enterprises. Public concerts in the new style were founded in many places in Germany. One of the oldest is that of Frankfurt (founded 1723 under Johann Chr. Bodinus); Leipzig followed, still under Bach's eye, with the Grosses Konzert (1743) that later became the Gewandhauskonzert (1781), and the Musikübende Gesellschaft (under Johann Adam Hiller from 1775 on). This last had been preceded by an organization of the same name in Berlin (under Johann Philipp Sack from 1745 on); the Spiritualkonzerte in that city (under Reichardt from 1783 on) acknowledge the French model in their very name. "The third period of the concert includes the years 1770–1800. It is the time when concerts spread to the middle-sized and small cities, the time in particular of the amateur concerts that from now on no city lacks." [35] In Vienna leadership fell to the *Tonkünstler-Sozietät* (founded 1771); this was followed by the concerts "auf der Mehlgrube" and "im Augarten," in which Mozart frequently appeared.

By the time of Haydn's late oratorios, the evolution of concert life had essentially reached its close, not only in Germany and Austria but in Europe generally; the types were firmly established and were not significantly altered in the 19th century, only carried

34. Preussner, *op. cit.,* p. 29 ff.
35. *Ibid.,* p. 32.

on. To public concert enterprises an enormous quantity of semipri-
vate concerts by societies and amateurs had been added. Traveling
virtuosos put on concerts in such numbers that they vied with each
other for position and success. Not only did the development end
around 1800, but the artistic and economic apex had been
reached; from that time on the decline of the concert is everywhere
lamented, and economic difficulties, at intervals gravely increased
in consequence of the Napoleonic wars, began to make themselves
felt. "A concert crisis exists so long as there are concerts." [36]

The early and the High Classic phases are therefore those
chapters of music history that developed the modern type of middle-class cultivation of music in the form of the public concert.
The 19th and 20th centuries took this product over with all its
strengths and weaknesses; essentially new forms of music-making
have not come up since. Beside the concert (in all its shades and
variations) only the opera still stood in the foreground of musical
interest during the Classic period. Church music carried on its traditional role without taking direct part in the new musical life. The
most vigorous and the most valuable center for the cultivation of
music, however, was now the house of the middle-class citizen,
where the new piano and chamber music as well as the song in all
its forms found their place, where music was made in the circle of
family and friends in a form that had not previously existed, where
children were educated in music not in a boarding school but by
private teaching. Here, in the last analysis, the true foundation was
laid upon which rested the entire practice of music in the Classic-
Romantic period: "Hausmusik," music-making in the home of
the amateur. Its importance for the evolving history of music cannot be overestimated. After the cultivation of music by court and
church of earlier times had been discontinued, only the interest of
the individual citizen could lay the further foundation of musical
activity. It was laid in the home, which has proved capable of
carrying this burden up to the present day.

With the development of the public concert, relations between
composer, performer, and consumer of music underwent funda-

36. *Ibid.*, p. 48.

mental changes. These changes, too, were in preparation during
the last phase of the Baroque,[37] but like the concert itself only became fully effective as classicism came into its maturity. In the Baroque, the musician as a rule had a fixed appointment that obligated him to compose as well as to perform. He was court, church,
or municipal musician, and in the society that employed him he
had his steady consumers and listeners. To this extent he had no
worries about the performances or the understanding of his works.
The social circle that surrounded and supported him formed a
unity with him, and in this unity music was not an optional cultural asset but a necessary function. So long as the musician himself kept to this arrangement and fulfilled the function assigned to
him, there could be no basic misunderstandings either between him
and his patrons or between composer and performer, because creator and performer were mostly still one and the same person or at
least belonged to the same closely circumscribed circle held together by unified views. In the last phase of the Baroque, a class of
more or less independent musicians—traveling virtuosos and those
opera composers who accepted commissions where they found them
—had only slowly come into existence; but they do not determine
the picture.

As concert life rapidly evolved, however, these relationships
crumbled away. Longest to endure was a certain unity between
creative and performing muscians: in the Classic era Italian and
German opera composers, symphonist of all schools, chamber-music and church-music composers still preferred to present their own
works; or else those who performed their music belonged to the
same social class. The professional composer who does not perform
and the practicing musician who does not compose first appeared
in Beethoven's day, and then for a long time only as the exception;
in the 19th century the above-mentioned unity still held in most
cases by far. Even the traveling virtuosos were as a rule the performers of their own works (as Abbé Volger and Paganini still
were, for example). The fact that in the Classic era, too, famous
musicians frequently still held regular appointive posts should not

37. Cf. Blume, *op. cit.*, Ch. VIII.

prevent us from realizing that in practice the relationship was changing more and more to that between Maecenas and independently creative artist. As in the public concert, so in the whole relationship between musician and society it soon becomes "a matter of indifference whether the patron is an individual gentleman of standing or the mixed public." [38] The Maecenas supports the musician, whether on a fixed salary or by commissioning compositions for which he pays; the artist fulfills these commissions less and less with regard to conventional forms and purposes, composing instead according to his own inspiration, pleasing or disappointing his patron and his audience with creations of an increasingly individual and original sort.

Criticism, unknown heretofore in this sense, waxes loud: criticism that concerns itself not much with the technical quality but rather with the individual and personal character of the work. Prince Esterházy now and then raised objections to the symphonies of his Kapellmeister Haydn, as did Archbishop Hieronymus Colloredo to those of his concert master W. A. Mozart; another Prince Esterházy took exception to the Mass he had commissioned from Beethoven, as Emperor Joseph II did to Mozart's treatment of the orchestra. If public professional criticism had become customary since the periodicals of Mattheson and Scheibe, there now began with Reichardt and Hiller a new sort of hermeneutic, i.e. interpretative, and often enthusiastic criticism that considered itself to be the mouthpiece of public opinion; on the one hand, "good taste" and the individual worth of the work of art should be brought to the public's attention, on the other, the creative artist and the performer should be instructed in the interest of what the critic considers the esthetic norm or what is agreeable to the public. And all this reflects nothing but the fact that the old social unity of the three segments of musical life has crumbled away.

In this process the musician more and more moves out of the Kapellmeister's relative seclusion into the spotlight of the podium; he exchanges the bond with rank and function for the dubious gift

38. In *Allgemeine musikalische Zeitung*, 1802 according to Preussner, *op. cit.*, p. 61.

of artistic freedom which brings him social independence and moral self-responsibility but also makes it necessary for him to assert himself daily. This readjustment took place very slowly, and very differently according to country, city, court, and, above all, personality, but it is everywhere to be detected. After the middle of the 18th century, the strict attachment to office and long-inherited forms of duty grows rarer, the musician becomes a personality with all social rights and privileges, his character clearly profiled, and frequently enters into a relationship of confidence with his patron (as for example Wagenseil, Dittersdorf, Haydn, and Beethoven did at times with theirs). The obligation, often formally specified, to reserve his compositions for the use of his own musical establishment is increasingly eased. His position in the hierarchy of officials and members of the court household gives way more and more to civic independence. In Leopold Mozart, an inculcated sense of order, strengthened by material worries, is in constant revolt against the fetters of office that seem to him no longer appropriate. Wilhelm Friedemann Bach, only slightly older, casts off the duties of an old-fashioned church position for the sake of a personal freedom to which he is not equal. Mozart definitely breaks with the social order of the *ancien régime,* enlightened as this was, changes over to an independent existence he believes warranted by his own capacities, and in the end suffers shipwreck in the conventional middle-class sense; and Mozart is probably the first composer in history of whose works a part at least met with no understanding from his contemporaries. Gluck belongs to the traveling conductor-composers and is one of the not so very few of this type who through their own attainments as composers managed to achieve a free artist's existence.

The life of Haydn provides the model for the whole subsequent development. He was for four decades Kapellmeister to the princely house of Esterházy, rose from a duty-bound official of the household to a ranking and personally highly esteemed "Herr Kapellmeister," was in practice independent from the 1780s on, was able to travel and to make what use he wished of his works despite a standing contract with the princely house, and in his old age lived a perfectly independent life. The princes he had served had long passed from orchestra owners to Maecenases, and occasionally to friends. The result of all this Beethoven inherited; Vienna's aristocracy felt called upon—without any sort of formal commitment, save the assurance of his remaining in Vienna when he threatened to go to Kassel—to support him for life. In Haydn's last years and in Mozart's the two opposite extremes of an artist's existence, as they were to be frequently repeated in the Romantic era, are already exemplified: both lived as free artists, but the one is the world-renowned master, everywhere acknowledged and treated as a matter of course with respect, sought after by public and publisher, knowing how to preserve his economic independence as well; the other, understood only with effort and achieving his ends only with difficulty, lives in a spiritual sphere that causes him to lose his footing in the material world.

From the musician's point of view, the freedom of the artist was the result made possible—but by no means attained or even striven for by all—by the decline of the old unity. From the consumer's point of view, things changed in the Classic period primarily in the sense that music was no longer an affair of social class and opportunity, but became a freely accessible cultural property. As an "amateur" he could take part in the countless choral societies or orchestras that were being formed; as an "expert," if he had the ability, he could rank with the professional musician in passing judgment; as member of the public he could for a consideration take passive part in every musical entertainment. The complete freedom of choice that distinguishes the Classic period presupposes the culture-hungry and educated public that supported public concerts, associations, clubs, and societies, the public music schools that were springing up, and many other institutions of musical life. It also presupposes the independent music publisher who on his own responsibility offers desired works of music for sale and helps guarantee the musician an independent living. The composer thus finds himself under the necessity of offering his works to the publisher; only few could boast, as Haydn in his last decades and Beethoven in 1800 were able to do, that their works were torn from their hands at any price. With this, too, came the interdependence of artistic creativity and commercial marketability unknown in earlier times but still in effect today.

In an age that had no legally established copyright (in 1794 the Prussian civil code for the first time defined reprinting as an infringement of another's property), this situation gave rise to countless abuses, from pirated editions to professional forgery; composers, publishers, and public have had to carry on ever-renewed battles for appropriate forms of copyright protection, up to the present. All in all the public, that is, the mass of music lovers, determined the market and therewith to no inconsiderable extent artistic creativity as well. The palmy days of this culture-loving public coincide exactly with the decades of the High Classic era. By around 1800 begins the complaint (since grown stereotyped) about "declining welfare, declining art, breadless and jobless composers." [39] With the Napoleonic wars, the 18th century's aristocratic and cultured ranks became impoverished; in Austria particularly an inflation of the currency cut deep into the musician's circumstances. While the Romantics, remote from all reality, dreamed up a blissful cloud-land of music, with the beginning of industrialization the way led mercilessly into materialism and to the modern mass society that has no inherent connection with the arts. The divergence here was now between the artistic understanding of elevated minds (easily diluted into "art-for-art's-sake") and the banality of the masses (bringing in its train the separation between "serious" and "entertainment" music). The harmonious unison of highest art and sheerest humanity was shattered, the dream of a universal language was over.

The Romantic period is the age of inner contradictions. In this age, whose select souls could not do enough in praise of the past and of everything ancient, most of the Gothic churches were torn down, and yet work on the Cologne cathedral continued to its completion. The insight that a breakdown between music and the broad masses must lead to ill luck for music and to a nihilistic emptiness in the industrialized masses had been achieved in all

39. Preussner, *op. cit.,* p. 98.

clarity in the Classic age. The necessity of working against such a collapse through deliberate education of the people had already been recognized by Pestalozzi, well pondered by men like Schiller, Goethe, and Wilhelm von Humboldt, and has busied intelligent brains ever since. It is no accident that from the 1780s on [40] serious efforts in behalf of popular musical education have never ceased. Great pedagogues and organizers of music entered upon the scene—J. F. Reichardt, J. A. P. Schulz, J. A. Hiller, H. G. Nägeli, C. A. Zeller, J. N. Forkel, and C. F. Zelter; Schultz and Zelter introduced into history the idea of music fostered by the state. At the historic moment when music and the people so happily came together, music experienced its deepest social crisis, the effects of which continue undiminished today.

As a result of the shift in social patronage of music to the level of the public, composers now no longer presented their works to a class in which they served as members; instead, as autonomous and responsible shapers of ideas valid for all humanity, they faced an amorphous multitude that they were to raise to their own sphere, to lift above itself, a public that was to worship them as demigods in the temple of art or to reject them as madmen. From the Classic era onward, to justify his own activity, to insure his own personal and artistic liberty in matters spiritual and material, became an inevitable challenge to the artist. The "free artist" (Haydn) of the Classic period must defend the dubious gift of freedom; the "bonded servant" (Haydn again) of musical organization in earlier societies had never been faced with this necessity.

Haydn had phrased the new situation with his incorruptibly temperate acumen in 1778: "The free arts and the so beautiful science of composition tolerate no shackling. Free the spirit and the soul must be if one would serve the widows and gather one's deserts." That is not only the striking renunciation of all old-style life of guild and office; the sentence also contains, taken quite literally, the justification of one's own acts. The artist who would be free

40. J. A. P. Schultz's memoir, *Über den Einfluss der Musik auf der Volksbildung* (On the Influence of Music on the Education of a People), 1790.

must "gather his deserts," and that means not only honors and distinctions but also money; nobody in those days recognized more clearly than Haydn the correlation of economic and artistic independence or knew so well how to profit by it. That is the material justification. The moral justification lies in the words "to serve the widows." For to the society that supports him and from which he has freed himself as an individual, the artist owes his freedom, while he voluntarily joins it again, in readiness to be socially helpful. Of this Haydn gives luminous examples in placing his works at the disposition of mankind not only as spiritual possessions but as a source of charity. The meaning of those words of his published shortly after his death (1810) by Griesinger—"It is not out of vanity, but the world may well know that I have not been a useless member of society and that through music one can also do good" —goes far beyond the trait of character it contributes to our picture of Haydn; basically it sums up the whole problem of the composer's free life as an artist in the Classic era.

In no other musician's personality did the original unity of creative achievement, Classic turn of the artist's mind, and form of social life manifest itself with such clarity as in Haydn. He developed the technique of composition to the final maturity of the Classical age, most convincingly exemplified the unison of highest art and highest aspirations of the people, and in his simple person embodied most purely the world-spanning humanity of music. His lesser contemporaries stand too far behind him in quality to bear comparison. In Mozart's most mature works the Classic is already darkened by the shadow of the Romantic. Beethoven in his work and personality embraces both the Classic and the Romantic. If there is a pure "classicism" in music, it is in the historical figure of Joseph Haydn that it became a perfected reality.

ROMANTIC MUSIC

I

The Beginnings of the
Romantic Era in Music

The noun "romanticism" and its adjective "romantic," stemming originally from 18th-century literature, have belonged since the beginning of the 19th century to the everyday vocabulary of music without ever having acquired a definitely circumscribed meaning. Even in musical historiography, they have become firmly entrenched, vague as their use has remained from the beginning until today and doubtful as it still is whether they really stand for a style, a technique, a formal canon, or merely a general artistic point of view, an intellectual attitude. It seems certain that they are not suited to delimiting an historical period.

The adjective "romantic" was used in 18th-century literature in the sense of "romance-like," "narrative." The corresponding noun is supposed to have first occurred in Novalis.[1] In music, too, the adjectival form seems to have been the earlier, and for a long time one still described things as "romantic" rather than attributing "romanticism" to them. Use of the substantive form to refer to a time, a manner, or an individual working in these did not become general in music until E. T. A. Hoffmann (1776–1822).

It is not certain when the adjective began to be associated with types or titles of compositions as a characterizing term. Since, at first consideration anyway, it does not imply a definite style or a definite tendency, this will be difficult to ascertain. Such concepts as "Romantic opera," "Romantic song," "Romantic piano piece,"

1. According to Peter Kluckhohn, *Das Ideengut der deutschen Romantik,* Halle, 1942, p. 29.

and the like did not spring up until later in the 19th century and
were first introduced by the newer musical historiography to de-
note comprehensive historical groups. In early times the adjective
was used now and again to indicate something about the content
or character of a literary or musical composition. Schiller called
his *Jungfrau von Orléans* (1802) a "romantic tragedy," Weber
his *Freischütz* (1820) a "romantic opera." In a similar sense, too,
Schiller in a letter to Goethe (June 28, 1796) speaks of *Wilhelm
Meisters Lehrjahren* as romantic, and this in view of its strange
happenings and of characters like Mignon and the Harper. To the
prevailing undertone of the work, in the sense of the unusual, were
presently added the alluring secondary tones: the chivalrous, the
antique or archaic, the basically naïve and folklike, the remote and
fabulous, the strange and surprising, soon, too, the nocturnal, the
ghostly, the frightful and terrifying—all these being of emotional
and imaginative content that readily becomes associated with the
concept of Romanticism, without necessarily always having to be
wholly or predominantly included therein. What makes "Romanticism" so difficult to grasp is just this: that now one quality dominates, now another, and to satisfy the concept, it is quite sufficient
if only one or just a few of these qualities are present. Schiller (in
a letter of June 26, 1797) calls a sketch of Goethe's for an epic
poem of the hunt "romantic," merely in the sense of "strange and
surprising." In those years, at any rate, discussion of what "Romantic" might really be, was already in full swing, even before any
attempts were made to separate "Classic" from "Romantic" con-
ceptually. Many passages in the Goethe-Schiller correspondence
imply how much the problem of the emerging Romanticism was in
the air, even though the concept itself and its antinomy to
Classicism were hardly ever called by name. By this same time, the
word has appeared in the musical sense. It is significant that Heinrich Christoph Koch's medium-sized *Dictionary* of 1807 contains a
small article "Romantisch," whereas in his voluminous *Lexikon* of
1802 the entry was still missing.[2]

In the decade between 1790 and 1800 the question of Roman-

2. Cf. *Classic Music*, p. 9.

ticism is countless times alluded to in literature as well as in music, and around 1800 German poets and composers were steeped in Romantic ideas. Friedrich Schlegel brought out his *Lucinde* in 1799, and about 1800 he began setting down his *Fragmente,* which were of such fundamental importance to the artistic view of the entire period. In 1796 Ludwig Tieck published a small book that more than any other gave wings to the ideas and the vocabulary of Romanticism: Wilhelm Heinrich Wackenroder's *Herzensergiessungen eines kunstliebenden Klosterbruders* (The Outpourings of the Heart of an Art-Loving Cloister-Brother), which also contained *Das merkwürdige musikalische Leben des Tonkünstlers Joseph Berglinger* (The Remarkable Musical Life of Joseph Berglinger, Composer). In 1799 he brought out the same author's *Phantasien über die Kunst für Freunde der Kunst* (Fantasies about Art for Friends of Art) with the musical allegory *Morgenländisches Märchen von einem nackten Heiligen* (Oriental Tale of a Naked Saint). Together in Nuremberg, the two friends had dreamed the dream of "old-German art." Wackenroder's writings introduced a religious note into the body of Romantic ideas on art and sought —as Goethe disapprovingly (and erroneously) expressed it (*Annalen,* 1802)—to establish "piety as the sole basis" of art. Tieck himself brought out in rapid succession, from 1799 on, his *Gestiefelte Kater* (Puss-in-Boots), *Sternbald, Musikalische Leiden und Freuden* (Musical Joys and Sorrows), and *Phantasus,* all more or less strongly impregnated with the Romantic idea of the close interweaving—indeed, the unity—of the arts and the conviction of the priority of music. In language, ideas, and imagery, Novalis with his poems (Schubert set some of the *Hymns to the Night*) and his novel-fragment *Heinrich von Ofterdingen* (1802) became a leader among the young Romantics; his mysticism, his inclination to dissolve the real and human in the imaginary and cosmic introduced into literature the enthusiastic tone of the transcendental. Music rises to the highest rank in the circle of the arts. In music the unutterable is spoken. It completes, perfects, in areas where the means of the plastic and the rhetorical arts come up against their own limitations.

These points of view and these endeavors lead, in the period 1780–1820, to a whole literature that stands on the boundary line between the arts, equally concerned with both sides of the border, and that, as regards music, numbers only a few professionally trained musicians among its authors, who are for the most part amateurs, poets, doctors, or philosophers. Even Johann Jakob Engel's *Über die musikalische Malerei* (On Musical Painting) of 1780 belongs in this category. Romantic self-mirroring and self-commiseration are already fully manifest in Friedrich von Dalberg's *Blicke eines Tonkünstlers in die Musik der Geister* (A Composer's Glimpses into the Music of the Spirits, 1787); the same author's *Vom Erfinden und Bilden* (Of Invention and Construction) and *Grundsätze der Ästhetik* (Fundamentals of Esthetics), both of 1791, are also worth noting. Wilhelm Heinse's novel *Ardinghello* (1787), laid in 16th-century Italy, is dedicated rather to the plastic arts and questions of general views on art, while his *Hildegard von Hohenthal* (1795–96) deals principally with questions concerning music in a pre- or early Romantic sense, though it also still poses some questions in the spirit of the Enlightenment. The strongest influence upon the entire Romantic movement from its beginnings to well into the 19th century, and quite particularly upon its musical views, was exercised by the novels, tales, and esthetic writings of Jean Paul—among others, *Hesperus* (1795); *Titan* (1800–03); especially *Flegeljahre* (Adolescence, 1804–05); *Vorschule der Ästhetik* (Introduction to Esthetics, 1804). They are steeped in music and exceed in their ecstatic enthusiasm and rapturous intensity of feeling anything that other Romantic writers have to say about that art.

What in Jean Paul and others moves along the "uncertain foundation" of dilettantist waywardness or ecstatic poetizing finds its synthesis—acute, critical, knowledgeably, but poetically conceived, and enlightened—in the writings of E. T. A. Hoffmann, the lawyer-jurist, who was poet, designer, composer, and conductor all in one person. These writings begin with *Ritter Gluck* (1809), and follow from then on in rapid succession: the *Kreisleriana,* musical reportage, reviews, etc., run on from 1810 for a decade, much of it

collected later in *Serapionsbrüder*. Among his last writings that
have something to do with music or are especially concerned with
it belong the *Lebensansichten des Katers Murr nebst fragmentar-
ischer Biographie des Kapellmeisters Kreisler* (Grumpy the Tom-
cat's Views on Life Together with a Fragmentary Biography of
Kapellmeister Kreisler), itself a fragment (1819–22), and the important *Nachträgliche Bemerkungen über Spontinis Oper Olympia*
(Supplementary Remarks on Spontini's Opera *Olympia,* 1821).
Though his own compositions disappoint the expectations aroused
by his esthetic views, yet it is undoubtedly Hoffmann who set the
stamp upon the Romantic concept of music in Germany, thence
also in France, and who definitively influenced Romantic thought
and feeling for a century. Caustic and fantastical, tearful and sarcastic, fleeing the world and yet sturdily of it, genuinely resigned
and feignedly ironic as he may reveal himself to be, there comes to
expression in his writings, pregnant and brilliantly formulated, all
that constitutes the very essence of the Romantic movement in
music. If there is yet a third much-read author who along with
Jean Paul and Hoffmann contributed to shaping the language,
ideas, and images of musical Romanticism, it is the musician Christian Friedrich Daniel Schubart, whose *Ideen zu einer Ästhetik der
Tonkunst* (Ideas on an Esthetic of Music, 1806) first published by
his son fifteen years after its author's death, already contains the
essence of the entire Romantic point of view on music and had the
greatest influence on Jean Paul as well as on Hoffmann.

The literature incontrovertibly shows that musical Romanticism began not, as is often stated, between 1810 and 1820, but simultaneously with literary Romanticism a couple of decades before
the turn of the century. All its definitive ideas were formed in the
18th century, and merely deepened and broadened in the following
decades. Hoffmann is no beginning, but rather an ending, if one
takes account of the first period of the movement. And musical
creativity in the spirit of these Romantic ideas began at the same
time. Romantic traits flare up in Johann Schobert's piano sonatas
(*c.* 1760). In German as in French compositions, we frequently
meet movement headings that stem from the rising Romantic vo-

cabulary, such as "with much feeling," "passionately," "agitated," and so forth.[3] C. P. E. Bach's late piano works (*Sonaten und freie Fantasien,* 1783–87) are examples of Romantic, almost Hoffmannesque fantasy. The improvised fantasies on which they were based must have been exemplary to a still higher degree, but even in the manuscript and printed editions they contain surprisingly "un-Classical" music, movements freely improvised on a grand scale and overflowingly expressive of deep feeling. To compare them to *Sturm und Drang* works in literature would be to undervalue them; one should rather understand them as closely related forerunners of Beethoven. Philipp Emanuel himself did not use the word "romantic" in his textbook (the two parts of which had already appeared in 1753 and 1762); like the word "classic," it was not yet usual in music. When either of these words occurs at so early a date, its meaning remains questionable, as in the case of the collection entitled *Tonstücke für das Clavier von Herrn C. Ph. E. Bach und einigen anderen klassischen Musikern* (Berlin, 1762), where "klassisch" probably means no more than "exemplary," "attractive," "charming"—and hence, in the last analysis, practically the same thing as "romantic." Although Mozart's work was, along with Haydn's, surely the epitome of "Classicism" in music, nonetheless it later took up in increasing measure—without ever abandoning this basic "Classic" approach—the alluring effects of somber colors, sudden changes of feeling, unexpected cloudings and clearings, enrapturing sensuality of sonorities and dusky irony. In doing this, it came so close, both in opera and instrumental music, to Romantic requirements that the Romantics themselves could without much deliberation construe it as Romantic.[4] To Tieck and Schlegel, Mozart became the Romantic par excellence.[5] Panegyrists of Mozart, like Jean Paul and Hoffmann, certainly often overshot the mark and thereby themselves contributed to the 19th

3. Cf. Barry S. Brook, *Simon Le Duc,* in *The Musical Quarterly,* XLVIII (1962), 498–513.

4. Cf. among others Leo Schrade in *Bericht über die musikwissenschaftliche Tagung,* Salzburg, 1931, Leipzig, 1932, p. 22 ff., and Hans Engel, *Mozart zwischen Rokoko und Romantik,* in *Mozart-Jahrbuch,* 1957, p. 63 ff.

5. Cf. MGG, article *Mozart,* 725, 751 f., 803 ff., 811 f.

century's misunderstanding of their idol. Yet their testimony does show spontaneous recognition of the psychic kinship, and however discolored, exaggerated, or exalted the Romantic picture of Mozart may have been, one cannot overlook the fact that without the basis of Romantic invention that actually informs Mozart's late works, this picture would not have come into existence. One should not underestimate the Romantic atmosphere that was spreading through music by the 1770s and '80s, and on the other hand one must take into account the fact that other causative impulses may also have participated in the romanticizing of the music of those decades. H. C. Robbins Landon has shown [6] that Mozart's G minor Symphony, K. 183, stems not simply from an individual need for romanticizing expression, but from a veritable family tree of ancestors. Barry S. Brook [7] calls attention to similar early romanticisms in French instrumental music.

One may well consider even Haydn's experimental symphonies (Nos. 39, 44–46, 49, 52; 1768–72) in the same connection. It is perhaps easier to draw parallels from them to the literary *Sturm und Drang* than from C. P. E. Bach, because they form an isolated group in Haydn's work and no apparent path leads from them to the Romantic era. If such a view proves correct, it still does not justify the drawing of a dividing line between such early phenomena and the Romantic period. We are dealing rather with an intermezzo in the course of development toward the Classic musical language, one that continued to work alongside and beneath the High Classic phase and eventually led to a kind of specifically Romantic musical language.[8] In choice of tonalities, rhythmic excitement, tense thematic work, motivic texture, predilection for unisons and harmonic jolts, these Haydn symphonies of around 1770 (whatever the reason for their being so constructed) anticipate much that we hear again in Beethoven.

The connections among these "early Romantic" events in musi-

6. *La Crise romantique dans la musique autrichienne vers 1770*, in *Colloques internationaux du Centre National de la Recherche Scientifique 1956*, Paris, 1958.
7. *Op. cit.*
8. Cf. *Classic Music*, p. 30 f.

cal creativity, as well as between them and the nascent Classic language of music, have hardly been looked into. Yet it is important
to remember that alongside the High Classic—and in spite of it—
there was, in music as in contemporary literature, such an early
phase of Romantic tendency (from the 1770s on, say, although
perhaps only in individual cases) before the Romantic movement
reached its high point after the turn of the century. Even Haydn's
late works are full of romanticisms: the string quartets after Op.
64 (1790), *The Creation* (1798), and *The Seasons* (1801). The
oratorios owe their decisive and lasting success not only to their religious delight in nature and their cosmopolitan language but also
very largely to their folklike, homely touches and atmospheric pictorial element. Goethe once especially praised the orchestral preludes in *The Creation*—from his viewpoint really an inconsistency
—while Schiller criticized the same work as "characterless mish-
mash", an involuntary testimony to its Romantic traits. Romantic
gloom or emotional indulgence, deviousness or irony lay much far-
ther from the straightforward and earthy Haydn than from Mozart.
This may explain why romanticisms occur as isolated effects in his
music, while Mozart's late work is romantically saturated at a
much deeper level. And yet a Haydn movement like the Adagio
(E major) from the G minor String Quartet Op. 74, No. 3 is not a
whit less Romantic than the Adagio movements of early Beethoven piano sonatas, and much more Romantic than the slow
movements of early Schubert symphonies. Classicism and Romanticism are simply interwoven inseparably with each other in Haydn
and Mozart, until Beethoven reveals the contrast and the unity in
the two and thus in some measure defines the antinomy. Despite
this opposition, Classicism and Romanticism continued to merge
into each other.

It was not only in the great masters that the springs of Romantic feeling welled up; the lesser and the least also played their part.
Our knowledge in this field is still but meager. There is no doubt
that many of Muzio Clementi's piano sonatas, caprices, and preludes of the 1780s and '90s, Johann Baptist Cramer's concertos
and other piano works of 1800–10 (the piano had about this time

become *the* Romantic instrument), Jan Ladislav Dussek's piano and chamber-music works of around 1800 sometimes speak an unmistakably Romantic tonal language, often at least a romanticizing one, and do so, like the compositions of the great masters, without giving up their basic Classic feeling. The same is true for several of the smaller composers such as Prince Louis Ferdinand of Prussia, Daniel Steibelt, Carl Czerny, Johann Nepomuk Hummel, Franz Ries, and others. Ernst Bücken's objection, that with these and other composers before and around Beethoven there is as yet no question of genuine Romantic music, only of occasional Romantic inspirations,[9] does not stand up, because the same may be said in a great many cases of the composers who were Romantic in the stricter sense, from Schubert to Mendelssohn, Eduard August Grell, Josef Gabriel Rheinberger, and others. How much of the music of the 19th century (even if one considers only that of Germany) is really "Romantic"? Just as in the 17th century not every sacred or profane composition, every Mass or motet was "Baroque," so in the 19th not every poem or every symphony, every drama or every opera was in the full sense "Romantic." Romanticism is no definable style but a spiritual attitude. The century brought forth avowedly a-Romantic, even anti-Romantic minds like Heine or Karl Ludwig Börne; among writers on music such various intellects as A. F. J. Thibaut, F.-J. Fétis, Otto Jahn, and —in a certain sense—August Wilhelm Ambros and Eduard Hanslick; among composers Sigismond Thalberg, for example, and Rossini, Offenbach, and Sir Arthur Sullivan.

Of course the question at once arises—and this holds for the Romantic era from its beginnings on into its last period—whether this picture is not distorted and whether the cause of the distortion is not to be sought in the underlying concept of Romantic here being too narrow. But if the concept is widened to include all the many counter- and undercurrents—the classisistic and the historicistic, the entertaining and the superficially brilliant, the realistic-naturalistic, the pathetic-monumental, and many others—then it is

9. Ernst Bücken, *Die Musik des 19ten Jahrhunderts,* Potsdam, 1929, p. 21 *et passim.*

stretched too far and becomes still less clear than it was to begin with. Unless we want to go so far as to declare the entire 19th century a "Romantic era" (commonly enough done in musical-historiography without inquiring in what measure name and content coincide), the concept should be delimited if it is to serve in deciding to what extent the century can be described as Romantic.

The Romantic musicians, at any rate, in no way thought of themselves as a strictly unified and historically delineated group with common aims in contradistinction to others (as, for example, the Renaissance musicians had done). Hoffmann freely counts Beethoven among the Romantics as well as Mozart, Haydn, and Gluck, but also Bach and (within limits) Handel. By doing this, he shows that he—himself a musician who understood his craft from the ground up—regarded Romanticism as not so much a matter of style or of forms but rather one of content and of musical shaping more or less dictated by feeling. Indeed the textbooks of the time, undisturbed by all the esthetic disputations, all problems of Classic and Romantic, show how solid was the common foundation on which composition rested. Heinrich Christoph Koch's *Versuch einer Anleitung zur Komposition* (1782–93), which Beethoven knew, Jérôme-Joseph de Momigny's *Cours complet d'harmonie et de composition* (1803–06), Anton Reicha's *Philosophisch-praktische Anmerkungen* (c. 1803) and *Cours de composition musicale* (1818), Gottfried Weber's *Versuch einer geordneten Theorie der Tonsetzkunst* (1817–21), Johann Bernhard Logier's *System der Musikwissenschaft und der praktischen Komposition* (1827), all bear witness—as do somewhat later Adolf Bernhard Marx's four-volume *Lehre von der musikalischen Komposition* (1837–47) in its countless editions (including a revision by Hugo Riemann), Johann Christian Lobe's four-volume *Lehrbuch der musikalischen Komposition* (1850–67), and Simon Sechter's three-volume *Grundsätze der musikalischen Komposition* (1857), which even Anton Bruckner studied—to the fact that before the tribunal of tidy craftsmanship, ardent emotions and esthetic alignments counted for little. Early or neo-Romantic, Wagnerite or Brahmsian, German, Czech, or Swede: for all of them it was the technical precepts that counted. They forged the strong link that held the musical creation of the period together until the 20th century, despite all its deeply divisive contradictions and widely divergent tendencies. In these precepts, Classic and Romantic were one and the same.

II

"Romantic" and "Classic":
The Romantic Concept in Music [10]

If in a conversation with Heinrich Voss (January 26, 1804) Goethe rejected "the distinction, now common, between Romantic and Classic" and held that "everything that is excellent is *eo ipso* Classic" (he again said the same to Eckermann, October 17, 1828), it becomes evident that despite earlier discussions with Schiller and the Schlegels the two words were not yet weighted with the sharply contrasting meaning they later acquired; rather, Goethe is here considering "a distinction between plastic and romantic as valid." On another occasion (in a conversation with F. W. Riemer, August 28, 1808) he sought to define Romanticism by its contrast with antiquity: if the latter deals with "the real," the former deals with the fantastic, the illusory; it is "delusive as a magic lantern picture"; the "tinge" of the marvelous, the sensuous, the untrammeled is recognizable. After Baron Oliva had played Beethoven for him, the famous conversation with Sulpice Boisserée took place (May 4, 1811) about Philip Otto Runge's allegorical representations: "beautiful and mad . . . , just like the Beethoven music that fellow plays, like our whole time."

It is significant that, as with Goethe, too, as soon as the Romantic is mentioned, music is quite spontaneously placed into relation with the other arts. The same conversation with Boisserée goes on "about the new fantastic essence, about the longing and restlessness, bursting all bounds and losing itself in the infinite, that is in music, in these experiments in painting, in philosophy,

10. Cf. *Classic Music,* Ch. II, pp. 8–17.

The Romantic Concept in Music

107

and in everything." Restlessness and longing—in these Goethe, too, sees the propulsive drives of Romanticism. Novalis and Schelling are mentioned; Goethe, at sixty-two, sees "the world falling to dust and back into its elements." His aim accurate as ever, he registers the characteristic features of the new movement. In another conversation with Boisserée (September 11, 1815) he reproaches the Romantic movement for showing "amid great merit and excellence, much decay."

Concerning his own share in analyzing the distinction between Classic and Romantic, his "objective approach" in contrast to the "subjective approach" of Schiller—who in his article *Über naive und sentimentalische Dichtung* had pointed out that he himself "was Romantic against his will," and how, following upon the Schlegelian polemics, the worldwide quarrel over "Classicism and Romanticism" came about "which fifty years ago nobody had thought of"—concerning all this Goethe expressed himself in his very old age (March 21, 1830) to Eckermann. A little earlier (December 16, 1829) he had once again explicitly stated that Classic and Romantic meant to him no irreconcilable opposites, that basically they indeed form a unity, inasmuch as, in the Helena act of *Faust,* Part II, he had led the two "poetic forms" out of their contrariety "as though up a rising terrain" to "a sort of reconciliation." Once, in a bad mood, he let fall the tart remark: "Classic I call what is healthy, Romantic what is sick" (to Eckermann, April 2 and similarly April 5, 1829); but here, too, he undoubtedly touched on a trait really present in Romanticism.

While for three or four decades Goethe sought always anew to achieve clarity with regard to the essence of Classic and Romantic, their contrast or their unity, he faced a younger generation during these same decades which was concerned not with clarifying concepts but with defending a program. In this generation the two concepts first begin to appear as fundamental opposites; in it Classicism first becomes suspect of being antiquated, pedantic, dry, savoring of cultivation, as against the Romantic spirit soaring in free fantasy. In opposition to Goethe's sober clarity and disciplined judgment Jean Paul, only fourteen years his junior, places pure

Romanticism, ecstatic abandon, the ardently sensual and emotional. Where the latter polemicizes against views on art that contradict his own, these views are of a type drawn from the arsenal of rationalism. His life's work revolves for the most part around music, and from him stems what Goethe called the "dissolution into the elemental" that became the desired ideal and the destiny of music. Scarcely anyone else, save possibly Hoffmann, contributed so definitively to shaping the Romantic concept of music, and no other poet had such a deep influence on composers and their production, up to the time of Schumann and the young Brahms, as Jean Paul.

Music now had no other task whatever than to proclaim man's inner nature, to voice the inexpressible. This is the creative artist's sole task, but he is in such measure obligated to this one task that he must sacrifice himself, extinguish his personality in his work (as happens with Wackenroder's Berglinger). The artist does not speak out of himself: something transcendent, other-worldly, universal speaks through him and out of him; he is the megaphone of the "world soul" (Novalis). The work of art dissolves into pure subjectivity and follows every stirring of the heart, tender or wild, to the point of the insipid, the tearful, and the morbid, to the reckless, the brutal, even to madness. Accordingly Jean Paul, like all later Romantics, at least in theory demanded the total subjection of form to content, indeed the annihilation of form by the fiery lava of temperamental outbursts. The problem of form-versus-content in Romantic music really goes back to him; he may to this extent be called the great antagonist of Goethe in all questions of musical esthetics. With him, too, began the romanticizing of Haydn and Mozart, whether in the misinterpretation of their music through the pathos of overwrought dramaticism and passion or in assessing their deliberate moderation as effeminacy. Every effort at a dialectically balanced judgment (such as Goethe always attempts) is lacking; judgment springs from stormy enthusiasm or flaming aversion, pious surrender of the heart or biting sarcasm of the intellect.

All the scintillating ingenuity and malicious brilliance of Romantic criticism have their origins here. Yet in this attitude there also comes to light a very generally valid trait of Romantic musical esthetics and music criticism: it is basically "dilettantish," in the sense that its starting point is not professional expertise but emotional experience. The 18th-century division of roles into artist, connoisseur, and amateur [11] is overturned. The prototype of listener and consumer of music becomes the "thinking enjoyer" (Goethe), and this category includes the music critic as well as the music esthetician, the concert-goer as well as the dilettante who makes his own music. In this new sense all are "dilettantes," not excepting those among the Romantic writers who (like Johann Friedrich Rochlitz, Hoffmann, Schumann, and the rest) were themselves professionally educated musicians, and this new attitude explains a number of reviews by Schumann, Ferdinand Ries, Liszt, *et al.,* that are otherwise difficult to understand. The opinions of such an amateur are just as subjectively conditioned as the composer's work of art, and where neither is sufficiently congruent there flares up the destructive biting criticism so frequently met with from Rochlitz through Hanslick up to George Bernard Shaw.

Significantly enough, Jean Paul by preference exemplifies his musical views from the works of Gluck, Haydn, Mozart, Reichardt, Spontini, or Grétry, or lesser masters like Wilhelm Rust, J. L. Schneider, Karl Siegmund von Seckendorff, and others. J. S. Bach he evidently did not know, and Beethoven, of whom he mentions only *Fidelio* and one symphony, he gladly avoids. In Jean Paul there also appears the leaning toward the folksong-like, the "artless," toward the primitive and antique, which then runs through the whole Romantic era as a sort of correlative to its most highly artistic inclinations, an echo of Herderesque tendencies, nourished on the songs—most unromantic but felt to be romantic —of Reichardt, Zelter, and others. Georg Schünemann [12] has instructively set forth how deeply Jean Paul's views are rooted in the

11. Cf. Arnold Schering, *Kritik des romantischen Musikbegriffs* in *Jahrbuch des Musikbibliothek Peters,* XLIV (1938), 9–23. (Also in *Vom musikalischen Kunstwerk,* Leipzig, 1949, p. 72 ff.)
12. In *Zeitschrift für Musikwissenschaft,* XVI (1934), especially pp. 461 ff.

past in all this, on what predecessors they are based, and how, inversely, ideas and concepts of the Enlightenment received from him their Romantic coloration; these relationships cast a special light upon the interlocking of rationalism and idealism in the music of the Romantic period.

Along with this, there appears a further, very characteristic side of the Romantic attitude to music that from the beginning of the 19th century until the present day has brought with it immeasurable consequences: its inclination to lean upon the music of a past that has become dear and to oppose to it in brusque antithesis a resolutely progressive and radically subversive modern music. Here again Beethoven becomes the dividing line between opinions. On the one hand his works were rejected as confused or highflown, and so remained unknown: Ludwig Spohr [13] tells of playing in 1804 at concerts in Leipzig and Berlin from the "new quartets" (i.e. Op. 18), which were still unknown in those two centers of music and which Bernhard Romberg ridiculed as "baroque stuff," while in France there had been no significant acquaintance with Beethoven's music before the famous performance of the "Eroica" by Habeneck in 1828.[14] On the other hand, they became, though not until much later, the beacons of an alleged musical revolution: Julius Becker in his novel *Die Neuromantiker* (1839), expressly traces a "new Romantic school" to Beethoven's late work.[15]

All the basic features of Romantic thinking about music are present in developed form by around 1800. They are now carried out, varied, and poeticized with glowing fantasy and passionate enthusiasm by writers in the first three decades of the 19th century. The sober Heinrich Christoph Koch can still say in his *Dictionary* of 1807: "Thus it is the character of the unusual, the great, and even the adventurous, embellished by charm, that determines the

13. *Selbstbibliographie,* Kassel, 1860–61, I, p. 85.
14. Cf. Leo Schrade, *Beethoven in France,* New Haven, 1942, especially Ch. I.
15. According to Schering, *Aus den Jugendjahren des musikalischen Neuromantik,* in his *Vom musikalischen Kunstwerk,* Leipzig, 1949, pp. 36–71.

nature of Romanticism." For men like Wackenroder, Tieck, Hoffmann, Carl Gustav Carus, the two Schlegels, music, being the most
"insubstantial" art, is also the most primary, "the original language
of Nature," "the spirit world of Djinnistan," as Hoffmann called it.
To Wackenroder, as even to Schopenhauer, it counts as purely
transcendental, the reflection of the infinite, as opposed to the
world of appearances. In the language of tones man understands
the language of the beasts, of the flowers, of the waters. In Jean
Paul and Hoffmann, natural scenes and fragrances merge into one
another with the awe of the beyond and the chords of the Aeolian
harp. The carnation's perfume induces in Kapellmeister Kreisler a
dreamy state, in which he thinks he hears the tones of the basset
horn swell and flow off again.[16]

In contrast to the exact "affections" of the French Enlightenment, music is understood as something altogether irreal, imaginary, an idea that penetrated German esthetics through English
writers like Charles Avison, the third Earl of Shaftesbury, and Edward Young. Hence music opens up the secrets of the cosmos, and
itself becomes a cosmic power. In rapturous descriptions of the un-
real, in the fabulous quality of all musical thinking, feeling, and
doing, and in the sense of oneness with the Infinite, Hoffmann
loses himself in buffoonery and nonsense. Kreisler in his madness
resolves on suicide and intends to "stab himself in the woods with
an augmented fifth"; he speaks of "snake-tongued sevenths" and
buys a garment "the color of which tends toward C-sharp minor,
so that to reassure spectators somewhat I am having a collar put
on in the color of E-major" (*Kreisleriana*). "Thus in a ghastly
manner his suffering became ludicrous." Only one capable of per-
fecting in himself such a complete synthesis of colors, pictures, and
sounds arrives at some notion of that Infinite which the genius in a
singular mixture of emotion, amazement, humility, self-awareness,
and self-irony approaches. The concept of music slumbering in the
universe itself is a sort of Romantic reawakening of archaic ideas
about the harmony of the spheres. "And the world begins to sing,

16. E. T. A. Hoffmann, *Höchst zerstreute Gedanken* (Highly Dis-
tracted Thoughts).

if you but find the magic word," says Eichendorff. Hence, too, it is
the "close-to-nature" instruments, the *Waldhorn* (natural horn),
the flute, the clarinet, that in Romantic lyrics sound from ruined
castles and enchanted gardens. The posthorn bears the yearning
soul afar on the wings of sound. Thoughts sublimated to this sort
of lyricism had been current as early as Herder's *Kalligone*
(1800). They were to find later development in the writings of
Robert Schumann.

The root of all music draws its strength from the "primal
sound" (*Urklang*), which is transformed into real sound by a secret
process. It lies with the artist whether he is able to awaken it and
give it form. Therefore the musician must feel at one with the
"All," he must experience the awe of the beyond through the voice
of Nature and must himself become the voice of the Universe. He
must not attempt to imitate natural sounds, scenes, experiences; all
imitation is, as is already the case with Goethe, strictly forbidden.
The idea of a symbolism that creates a secret link between the subject and its representation [17] was worked out in the utmost variety
by the Romantics. An inexplicable inspiration enables the composer to express in his work that which flows to him from the
springs of the Infinite and to shape this "content" without any admixture of intent and purpose simply by the power of his creative
faculties. In the process he foregoes all descriptiveness and every
brilliant effect, and pours what he has received into his work
through the medium of his personality, in pure form and without
residue—this is his highest task.

Hence the performing artist, too, must subordinate himself ut-
terly to the will of the created work and must "disdain to make *his
own* personality count in any way," as Hoffmann puts it in his
Beethovens Instrumentalmusik; here the idea of "loyalty to the
work" (*Werktreue*) finds its expression, presumably for the first
time, and simultaneously its deeper motivation. Thus the utmost
subjectivity becomes the high-priestly service to the Infinite. Every
admixture of other motives—contemplative ideas, pictorial presentations, descriptive paintings, narration—every program, in short,

17. Cf. *Classic Music,* p. 13.

but also in the end every literary text, besmirches the work of art, which in the most exalted cases becomes "absolute" music (Hoffmann). For this reason, now for the first time in history, pure instrumental music stands above every other.

If these aims are achieved, then music is "the most Romantic of all arts, one might almost say: the only one that is genuinely Romantic, for only the Infinite is its subject" (Hoffmann again). To free himself from disordered fantasy and speak a comprehensible language, the composer nevertheless needs the techniques and forms of composition; he even needs certain generally understandable symbols for feelings and values, which will prevent him from sinking into the sibylline, as Beethoven is so often reproached for doing in his late works. But here the Romantic composer finds himself in the ever-present dilemma between the inspiration flowing into his creative work as pure "content" and the "form" he needs for shaping it into a work of art.[18] Fundamentally the entire esthetic of Romantic music circles about this cleavage, from the beginnings up to Wagner, Pfitzner, and even to the present, where it comes up again, strangely befogged, in Stravinsky's *Poetics of Music*.

The way to a perfectly "pure" music was laid by the Classics: the comparison Hoffmann draws (*Beethovens Instrumentalmusik*) between Haydn, Mozart, and Beethoven is highly instructive. Haydn stands upon the threshold that leads to the portals of Romanticism. Mozart, not understood in his day, inaugurates the Romantic era; *Don Giovanni* is a Romantic opera (*Don Juan* and Spontini's "*Olympia*"). Mozart's High Romanticism will of course be understood only by those who have studied "older, energetic works" (in his review of Gluck's *Iphigénie*); Mozart's music leads them "into the depths of the spirit-world," to an "awareness of the Infinite." [19] Beethoven was the first, however, who was able "to open up the realm of the immense and awful," in the sounds of which "the pain of infinite longing . . . and every desire . . . sinks

18. Form in the widest sense of the word (cf. MGG, article *Form*, 523–38).
19. Hoffmann's review of Beethoven's Fifth Symphony; cf. also his letter to Hippel of March 4, 1795.

away and ceases to exist"; in this realm of wrestling passions "we live on, far-withdrawn, beholders of spirits." Beethoven's music "awakens just that very infinite longing which is the essence of Romanticism" (*Beethovens Instrumentalmusik*). Only the genius is able to overcome the contradiction between such power and "the mathematical proportions that to the grammarian remain . . . but dead, rigid examples in arithmetic," and to transmogrify the elementary forms of music into "magical compounds out of which he causes his enchanted world to rise" (in his review of Beethoven's Trio, Op. 70, No. 1).

Under the influence of conceptions of this sort, J. S. Bach is romanticized into a mystic and a Gothic artist; his music stands in relation to that of the old Italians (Jacopo Antonio Perti and Orazio Benevoli are mentioned) "as the Cathedral in Strasbourg to St. Peter's in Rome," and his counterpoint becomes "thrillingly secretive combinations," oddly intertwined mosses and herbs, veins in rock, "a Sanskrit of Nature expressed in tones" (*Höchst zerstreute Gedanken*). How far idealistic esthetics had here departed from basic reality is evident from a glance at the textbooks of Fux and Albrechtsberger, which after all underlie contemporary composition and to which composers had of necessity to find their way back out of their dream world. How long this dilemma continued to exist is illustrated almost a hundred years later by Bruckner's testy remark: "Counterpoint is not a matter of genius, but a means to an end." [20] Older Italian church music is held to be simple, pious, unproblematical, the model of "true church music." Any sort of historical view of older music is still totally lacking. It is loved for its "purity," with which it fulfills an oft-repeated basic requirement of the Romantics. A. F. J. Thibaut's *Reinheit der Tonkunst* (On Purity in the Art of Music) was reprinted over and over again between 1825 and 1861, not least for the reason that this little book accurately reflects the Romantic attitude toward older music in the spirit of those contemporary "Nazarene" painters who sought to restore to Christian art its medieval purity. Hoffmann himself made an important contribution to this theme with

20. In a letter to F. Bayer, April 22, 1893.

his article *Alte und neue Kirchenmusik*,[21] and in practice both Catholic and Protestant efforts at church-music reform, like those of Cecilianism [22] later, did homage to this same ideal program.

Romantic musical esthetics, with all its striving for a new humanity, a new truth and immediacy in music and musical understanding, is above all to be grasped as springing from the reaction against the esthetics of the Enlightenment represented by Batteux and his school, a reaction set afoot in part by Rousseau, in part also by the English school (Shaftesbury, *et al.*), and which found its deeper grounding in Fichte and Schelling. It never itself realized how much of the Enlightenment it still contained, how inherently contradictory it was, and to what extent it was but a variant of musical Classicism. It prescribed and romanticized out of hand everything that suited it in contemporary or slightly earlier musical composition and even in that of a more remote past, regarding the latter as something of its own, something "romantic," without drawing any boundaries, historical, formal, or stylistic. To Hoffmann, even Palestrina could on occasion be "romantic"; Bettina von Arnim could resolutely reject the songs of Zelter and Reichardt as "music of the Enlightenment." On the other hand, however, this Romantic esthetic set up with surprising speed a barrier against the new music of its own time, the moment this music was felt to be unorganic, sophisticated, oversmart, striving for effect, or, again, flat, empty, superficial. Carl Gustav Carus spotted a sign of decline in Beethoven's Ninth Symphony, Hoffmann criticized the *Missa solemnis* for its "glare and motley."

If a composition does not fulfill the highest (and that to the Romantics means at the same time the most subjective) demands of the critic, the reproach of epigonism is quickly at hand (Hoffmann, for example, raised it against Cherubini), a reproach that constantly recurs in the criticisms and reviews of Schumann, Berlioz, Liszt, Wagner, Eduard Hanslick, Hugo Wolf, and others. It positively poisoned the 19th century. The cult of artistic originality

21. At first with reference to Beethoven's Mass in C, in *Allgemeine musikalische Zeitung,* 1814; later included in *Serapionsbrüder.*
22. Cf. *Classic Music,* p. 4.

is so overdriven that it falls back upon itself and, formulated as a
radical demand, demolishes every scale of values. What is truly
original (like the last works of Beethoven, for example, and later
those of Wagner and Bruckner) is decried as high-flown fantasy,
the mediocre lauded as model for a canon of beauty, the use of
which naturally led to countless misjudgments. In opposition to the
new, older composers like C. P. E. Bach, Georg Benda, Ernst Wilhelm Wolf, Hasse, Jommelli, Traetta, and others are now cited as
great masters of the past and models for the present. Thus new
and old, enthusiasm and criticism, ideal and reality, emotion and
good sense fell ever deeper into inextricable contradiction.[23]

The image of the musician who suffers through himself, his
life, and his art never faded, from the time of Beethoven's Heiligenstadt testament (1802) up to Bruckner, Mahler, and Pfitzner.
Called to the highest task, consecrated priest and seer, bound to
the ordinary, obligated to reality, the artist ends up antagonistic toward himself and the world in which he lives. The society which
he faces as herald of eternal values and to which he must make
himself comprehensible through the banal resources of convention,
does not understand him and mocks him where it does not shyly
honor him. He is no longer the equal of its members; he has
stepped out of the circle in which heretofore he had been at home.
The crumbling of relations between artist and public, between art
and the crowd of the small-minded, is past arresting. Hoffmann's
Kapellmeister Kreisler endures "hellish torture" when he comes up
against the superficiality of bourgeois society (*Musikalische Leiden,* published in 1810). He defends himself with diabolic sarcasm, reflecting upon his own superiority. But this society will not
put up with him. He seeks refuge in solitude and in Bach's *Goldberg Variations,* that is, in a beloved past.[24] Only a Romantic disposition can enter into Romanticism; only the poetically exalted

23. E. T. A. Hoffmann, *Der Musikfeind* (The Enemy of Music), first
published in 1814.
24. Similarly polemical and critical of society is Hoffmann's *Nachricht
von einem gebildeten jungen Manne* (Report of a Cultured Young Man).
The same thought, in the form of lyric resignation, is to be found in Franz
Schubert's poem *Gebet* of 1823.

spirit, consecrated in the temple's center, can understand what the consecrated one is saying in his ecstasy (*Kreislers Lehrbrief,* 1814). But the reality looked quite different, and in its antagonism to that reality Romanticism's ardor of genius was shattered.

The high-strung Romantic concept of music was rooted in a sort of confession of faith: in the circle of the arts music takes the lead. Superior to all the other arts through its "immateriality," pure spirit, expression of the "inmost self" (Hegel), or image of the will (Schopenhauer), it can, as no other utterance of the human mind, guide the soul toward the Infinite. In music the contradiction between finite and infinite is cancelled out and man finds salvation in his purer self.

This concept of music was complete in itself and fully rounded; it was not to undergo further development. It continues to underlie, with modifications, the writings of Schumann, Liszt, Wagner, and many others, up to Pfitzner, experiencing many qualifications and pertinent modifications,[25] but remaining fundamentally unaltered. When Carl Maria von Weber describes the basis of all musical creation as "that undefined yearning toward dark distance from which one hopes for relief . . . that painful wrestling of inner forces, a struggle oppressively fettered by consciousness of the high idea, . . . this chaos of surging, distressful feelings" (*Tonkünstlers Leben, c.* 1820), he is merely putting into words what all his contemporaries felt, and thus comes close to Hoffmann. When Robert Schumann pictures his course [26] as "a rather lonely one, along which no hurrah from a great company gladdens my working, upon which only my great models Bach and Beethoven look at me and see to it . . . that words of comfort are not lacking," he is expressing a view of the artist and his position in society that is found as early as Hoffmann and as late as Pfitzner. And when Wagner writes: "What makes me love music so unutterably is that it keeps everything secret while it says the most un-

25. Ferdinand Hand, *Ästhetik der Tonkunst,* Leipzig, 1847 (translated into English by W. E. Lawson, London, 1880) and later Eduard Hanslick, *Vom Musikalisch-Schönen* (The Beautiful in Music), 1854 (modern reprint, Wiesbaden, 1966).
26. Letter to Simonin de Sire, February 8, 1838.

thinkable things; this makes it, literally, the only true art," [27] he is
using, to express the rank and the capabilities of music, words that
half a century earlier Jean Paul or Hoffmann might well have
used. Again, when Richard Strauss still finds it necessary to explain with regard to his symphonic tone-poems: "For me the poetic program is nothing more than the constructive inducement the
forms offer for expression and for the purely musical development
of my feelings," [28] he is taking exactly the same position toward
the problem of program music that we have already read of in
Hoffmann, Schumann, Wagner, and others. Finally, when in 1919
Hans Pfitzner states that "Inspiration is the essence of music as a
creative art" and that "music is simply the purest, most genuine,
and strongest art expressive of mood," [29] a whole century of Romantic thought on music comes to life again in his definitions.

Firmly founded on German idealism, this Romantic concept of
music has remained basically unaltered up into the 20th century,
despite all gradations, variants, and countercurrents. From Germany it spread to other countries, above all to France and the
Eastern European nations. In France the strongest influence was
exerted by Hoffmann; [30] in the writings of Berlioz, George Sand,
F. de Lamennais, Eugène Delacroix, Alexandre-Étienne Choron,
François-Henri Castil-Blaze, Émile Deschamps, Jean-Baptiste Sa-
batier, Hippolyte Barbedette, and beyond, traces of the German
Romantic view of music continued to have effect in that country
well into the present century.[31]

Even though in Germany itself the Romantic movement in the
narrower sense, which one may call the "High Romantic," soon

27. Letter to Princess Karoline Wittgenstein, April 12, 1858.
28. Franz Trenner, *Richard Strauss, Dokumente seines Lebens und
Schaffens*, Munich, 1954, p. 96; from Strauss's letter to Romain Rolland of
July 5, 1905.
29. *Die neue Ästhetik der musikalischen Impotenz*, 1919, pp. 109 and
147 respectively.
30. Cf. among others Hans Eckardt, *Die Musikauffassung der französischen Romantik*, dissertation, Heidelberg, 1932; Léon Guichard, *La musique et les lettres au temps du romantisme*, Paris, 1955; Hans Puls, *Die
Musikauffassung der französischen Romantiker*, dissertation, Saarbrücken,
1956.
31. For Russia, cf. Frank Siegmann, *Die Musik im Leben und Schaffen
der russischen Romantiker*, Berlin, 1954.

began to fade, and though together with the "Junges Deutschland" and "Jeune France" movements a second phase began in both Germany and France that is usually called "neo-Romantic," the basic principles were not changed. Neo-Romanticism introduced two tendencies, neither of them basically new but both now prominent in the foreground. One is the half-real, half-pretended anti-bourgeois rebelliousness that found expression—frequent and powerful, often grotesque or satirical, but often, too, ironic and self-mocking—in revolutionary or at least counter-Philistine writings, proclamations, compositions, and program explanations, especially in Robert Schumann's circle of the *Neue Zeitschrift für Musik* (after 1834). At times this rebelliousness was also sharply directed against the older Romantic period, as for example, when Wagner in one of his early articles (*Über die deutsche Oper,* 1834) attacked that idol of the earlier Romantics, Weber's *Euryanthe*. In a similar attitude of revolutionary criticism J. L. Wienbarg, lecturer at the University of Kiel, conducted his *Ästhetische Feldzüge* (Esthetic Campaigns, 1834), while this rebellious romantic literature reached a peak in Wagner's writings on revolution, e. g. his *Art and Revolution* of 1849. Composers became anarchists, Wagner a friend of Bakunin. It was an intoxicating Utopia that these people conjured up. The fiery breath of this new dawn lent wings also to Berlioz and the young Liszt.

But despite the deep seriousness and idealistic devotion that animated the movement, it rapidly faded away. By 1844 Hermann Hirschbach, looking back in his *Musik-kritisches Reportorium,* regards neo-Romanticism as played out, submerged.[32] It had set for itself high goals; it had wanted to stir people up; it had raised its banner in battle against the "peaceful dreaminess" to which most of its contemporaries only too easily surrendered. It had awakened an optimistic belief in progress. An attendant phenomenon, it is true, was the tendency of composers to lean more and more heavily on Bach on the one hand, Beethoven on the other, while the Classic masters (in the narrower sense) lost standing. In the 1830s Mozart's works slowly passed into the background of interest; in

32. According to Schering, *Aus den Jugendjahren . . . ,* p. 70.

1841 Schumann made his famous remark to the effect that Haydn
seemed like "an old friend of the family" and had "nothing new"
to say. Mozart now ranks as "the most objective [i.e. the most
unromantic] of all composers"; things are now carried to the point
of that Apollonian glorification of his genius which Otto Jahn then
seized upon and in his portrait of Mozart diluted to a spotless, altogether classicistic perfection.[33] Haydn's symphonies gradually
disappeared from concert programs, as Mozart's stage works did
from the repertory of opera houses. "In 1848 Moritz Hauptmann,
Robert Franz and the young Hans von Bülow were unanimous in
ranking his [Mozart's] Requiem after Luigi Cherubini's 'much
grander' work." [34]

Historically the most important result of the new movement,
however, and at the same time the most lasting, was the provocative, inflammatory, often violent character of many of its artistic
products. Here it pointed to really "Neue Bahnen" (New Ways—
the title of the article by which Schumann introduced the young
Brahms), here it battled against Philistinism, here it revealed once
more the powerful idealistic drive that flowed into it from the primal Romantic conviction of music's leading position in the realm
of the spirit and of its direct derivation from the Infinite. Schumann's Op. 1 appeared in 1830. Chopin began concertizing with
his own piano works in 1829. Berlioz's *Symphonie fantastique* had
its first performance in 1830. Liszt's first piano works appeared in
print during the 1830s. All these exerted an immeasurable influence on contemporaries and followers, and a considerable portion
of the works of these "neo-Romantics" has survived beyond the
middle of the 20th century, indeed, together with the more specifically "Classical" repertory, still forms at the present time the basis
of concert programs in all countries. Then when Wagner's operas
—*Rienzi* (1842), *Der fliegende Holländer* (1843), *Tannhäuser*
(1845)—began their triumphal progress in Germany, a large part
of the musical theater was swept into the neo-Romantic move-

33. In the years 1856 ff.; cf. MGG, article *Mozart*, 808.
34. Schering, *Aus den Jugenjahren* . . . , p. 55, after Bülow, *Briefe*, I,
p. 138.

ment, while on the other hand the contrast with the classicistic, thoroughly anti-Romantic musical theater of Bellini, Donizetti, Rossini, and the young Verdi was intensified with extreme sharpness.

But it is not to be denied that what here conquered the world with such tempestuous ardor was a number of individual personalities and anything but a unified school. They obeyed the law of subjectivism, which had brought them to the fore, in that each one followed his own daemon. This explains why the neo-Romantic period, in the very time of its dissolution, developed its highest radiance, sending forth in the second half of the 19th century a plethora of contradictory phenomena, of individual ideas and talents, but in the process losing more and more any stamp of stylistic unity. There is no other period in music in which the contradictions are so clearly defined, directions diverge so sharply, and that has so little in the way of an obligatory, central model to guide it as the second half of the 19th century. If one still wishes to call it Romantic (as has become customary), one must at least remain aware that the only unity left is in the name.

The second tendency introduced with neo-Romanticism lay in the spread of apparently anti-Romantic inclinations and alignments. Among them belongs the brilliant virtuosity that grew up at this time. Since 1830 Paganini had been conquering all Europe with his daemonic tricks; a little later Charles-Auguste de Bériot and other fiddlers began their virtuoso concert tours. Prima donnas like Henriette Sontag and Maria Felicità Malibran-García had the musical public of the world at their feet. At around this time Friedrich Kalkbrenner and Sigismond Thalberg were garnering their first sweeping pianistic successes in Paris. Around 1830, too, the very opposite of virtuoso brilliance—namely historicism, and with it a historical interest—acquired a foothold in the practical cultivation of music, and research was directed toward opening up the past. Giuseppe Baïni's *Palestrina* appeared in 1828. In 1829 Mendelssohn performed Bach's *St. Matthew Passion* in Berlin, a hundred years after it was written. In the same year studies in early Netherlandish music began with the important essays of Ra-

phael Georg Kiesewetter and François-Joseph Fétis. Again, at the
same time, but very quietly, a spring welled forth that was immediately to become a stream and flood the whole realm of music in an
unprecedented manner, up to the present day. Since the 1820s the
Viennese waltzes of Joseph Lanner and Johann Strauss the Elder
had achieved extraordinarily widespread distribution. The entertainment music that developed from here, at first on a high artistic
level, later ran out on a plane lower than music history had ever
known.

These and other anti-Romantic efforts and tendencies contributed a great deal to the decay of Romanticism and, in association
with the revolutionary subjectivism of esthetic judgment and the
unimpeded autonomy of the individual artist, led to boundless freedom and unlimited self-assertion, which saw its final goal in the
unshackled fulfillment of personality. That only genius itself was
entitled to lay down its own laws became an article of faith of the
"late Romantic period," if one wishes to include the late 19th and
early 20th centuries in some single historical characterization.
From Richard Wagner to Richard Strauss, innumerable writings
and letters of creative musicians bear witness that it is only the
free artistic will of the individual that determines direction and
shaping, sound patterns and forms, performance and use of a
work, to which the consumer of music must subject himself
unquestioningly. Never before had music history known conditions
of such confusing abundance and capricious variety, and no earlier
period is stamped with such a chaos of contradictions as this.[35]
The so-called "late Romantic period" was a time of limitless possibilities, but also of total dissolution in irresponsible heterogeneity
of a musical thinking that had lost every binding ideal. At all other
times in music history, however varied and however contradictory
its products, everyone was bound by configurations and forms
within certain limits and valid for all. In the declining old age of
"Romanticism," the formerly unifying concept of music faded, suc-
cumbing to the claims of the individual. The predominant subjec-

35. Cf. Friedrich Blume, *Die Musik von 1830 bis 1914* in *Musica,* XVI
(1962), 283–91, and in *Kongressbericht,* Kassel, 1962.

tivism was part of its nature from the very beginning; now it had thrown down all barriers, had indeed battered the unity of the period to pieces. The Romantic era was dead. The generation that came on the scene around 1910–20 found itself faced with the ruins.

III

The Romantic Era as an Epoch in Music History

Classicism and Romanticism, then, form a unity in music history. They are two aspects of the same musical phenomenon just as they are two aspects of one and the same historical period. Within this musical phenomenon as within this period—and, indeed, from their beginnings to their gradual termination in the 20th century—there ran currents that were now more classicizing, now more romanticizing. These currents cannot be classified, because they were dependent on personalities, tendencies, fashions, and objectives. The basic tasks and trends in which the musicians of this period saw themselves involved always remained the same, as did their basic understanding of the nature of music, despite all more or less positive counter-, under-, and side-currents. There is accordingly no "Romantic style" as such, the way there are definable and delimitable styles for other periods of music history. There is only a slow transforming of the stylistic type that had taken shape at the beginning of the Classic-Romantic age [36] and from there on had evolved, intensified, been complicated, differentiated again, overworked, and finally disintegrated, just as had been the case in other periods of music history—the Renaissance, the Baroque. And just as the Baroque had begun by renouncing the immediate past yet had nevertheless carried on the substance of that past partly unchanged, partly recast to the new age's needs in sonority and form, so after about 1920, with Stravinsky, Bartók, Hindemith, Schoenberg, and Webern, a "new

36. Cf. *Classic Music,* p. 30 f.

music" began by a renunciation but has carried on the surviving substance of Classic-Romantic music up to the present—now in countless continuing forms and configurations, now recast into something of its own. The beginnings of great epochs in music history can be determined, if one takes heed of the arising new and turns away from the still lingering old; but their endings cannot be defined because each epoch lives on under that which follows it.

The unity of Classicism with Romanticism is so pronounced that basically there is neither a purely Classic nor a purely Romantic period. What appears in Haydn and Mozart as the fullest maturity of Classicism is permeated with the provocative charms of Romanticism. These it is that lend the "Classic style" that indescribable atmosphere of characterful sensuousness, of the unique and the "infinite," which constitutes the essence of High Classicism, while what appears in Schumann or Brahms as most sublimely Romantic rests firmly on the underpinnings of this "Classic style." Not until Romanticism's "blue flower" blossomed in the pure mountain air of Classicism did its music come to perfection in the highest classicity. Where in the very early Classic period this interpenetration is still lacking, something cool, stern clings to its musical works, as in those songs of Zelter or of Reichardt that Bettina von Arnim for this very reason rejected as "smacking of the Enlightenment." What they miss is, in Koch's definition,[37] "the uncommon, the great, the daring even, beautified by graciousness" in which he sees the essence of Romanticism but in which today's view of history sees the essence of the Classic-Romantic style. Not until Romanticism's charms have worked their way into the clear severity of the Classic style's forms do we get that which in Haydn and Mozart perforce won over their contemporaries as well as their followers, a style breathed upon by the Romantic spirit and that we, looking back from the 20th century, call the "High Classic" style.[38] The Romantic era never coined a divergent and independent style; it simply continued to further shape this High Classic type.

37. *Ibid.,* p. 8 f.
38. *Ibid.,* p. 30 f.

"Stylistic criticism of romantic music offers the greatest difficulties to musicology. . . . On the one hand romantic music clings to the formal stylistic factors of classicism, on the other it seeks to eradicate boundaries and architectural logic. The loosening and flexibility of the coloristic, freely unfolding melody, the differentiated harmony, rich in dissonances and leaning to a veiling of tonal relationship, resulted in a wide variety of refined tonal and sonorous sense; the immensely enriched rhythm, lending itself to many combinations and indulging in the reversal of strong and weak beats, the intimate, egocentric, dreamy, oscillating and fantastic mood complexes, all created a conflict not only with classicism but within the romantic style itself." [39] Even that which we ordinarily call the "Romantic" element in music is in itself full of cleavages and contradictions. "We seek in vain an unequivocal idea of the nature of musical Romanticism." [40]

The Romantic quality that characterizes Schubert is different from that in Mendelssohn or Brahms, to say nothing of Dvořák or Grieg, Moussorgsky or Falla. The Romantic quality in Beethoven's music inspired Berlioz and Pfitzner to the same degree, indeed, but in so doing it brought forth results that are similar in only one respect: that which in Berlioz and Pfitzner is not Romantic, namely, their inherited Classical canon of elements and forms. This canon, which remained basically the same from Stamitz to Reger, distinguishes all musical production of the Classic-Romantic period from that of the late Baroque as well as from that of twelve-tone or serial music. But within the Classic-Romantic period it remains the obligatory and unifying norm to which Bruckner goes back as well as César Franck, Vaughan Williams as well as Tchaikovsky, Wagner as well as Verdi. To this extent one may well define a Classic-Romantic age as an entity, distinct both from the preceding Baroque age and (though in this case not very clearly) from the succeeding "New Music"—but not a Classic age as distinct from a Romantic. [41]

39. Paul Henry Lang, *Music in Western Civilization*, New York, 1941, p. 816.
40. Alfred Einstein, *Music in the Romantic Era*, New York, 1947, p. 4.
41. Cf. *Classic Music*, p. 16 f.

Upon this canon, this style-norm of the Classic-Romantic period, these men all rest, however divergently they developed their individual worlds of sonority and form, tonality and texture, expressive intent and forcefulness of statement: Strauss, Reger and Pfitzner, Smetana, Dvořák and Janáček, Mascagni, Puccini, and Malipiero; by this canon even Gershwin and Menotti stand or fall, Burkhard and Sutermeister, Walton and Britten, Prokofiev and most of Stravinsky, Schreker and Hindemith, Falla and Granados, Milhaud and Honegger, just as Mozart and Beethoven, its creators, rested upon it. It is the epoch-making force before which the distinction between "relatively Classic" (i.e. classistic) and "relatively Romantic" (romanticistic) sinks to the level of a subordinate question of subjective judgment. Even though it was only this canon of forms and elements [42] that held the age together it nevertheless guaranteed a certain unity in the period in the face of its widely divergent tendencies and individualities. Alfred Einstein's aphorism "Romanticism hates Classicism" [43] can claim only a much qualified validity, and such allegedly inimical brothers as Hanslick and Wagner, Bruckner and Brahms, Pfitzner and Paul Bekker appear in retrospect to be sons of the same mother.

In the face of this ultimate unity, too, every attempt to split the period from (roughly) 1770 to 1920 into a Classic and a Romantic phase, however organized, deteriorates into a purely extrinsic temporal measurement, and the question so often and so passionately discussed, whether Beethoven should be counted among the Classics or the Romantics, becomes meaningless. He was simply both in his own personal way, just as all creative musicians were, from Philipp Emanuel Bach and Haydn to Strauss and Reger, each in his own unique and particular manner. Beethoven was able to be both because Classic and Romantic are one; only the emphasis shifts, now to this side, now to that. Beethoven was far more Romantic than Mozart, Schubert, Mendelssohn, or Brahms, at least in a large part of his works, if one takes the word "Romantic" in the

42. Tonality, harmony, metric and rhythmic treatment, etc.; cf. *Classic Music*, p. 30 ff.
43. *Op. cit.*, p. 4.

sense in which Hoffmann and his contemporaries understood it, and with his late works he pointed the way for the neo-Romantics, for Wagner, Liszt, and many younger composers. But at the same time he embodied that Classic-Romantic canon of form, the style-type of his period, with such extraordinary determination and such radiance that he could become the central figure of the 19th century to a much higher degree than Haydn and Mozart. That is why the novelist Robert Griepenkerl, in *Das Musikfest oder die Beethovener* (The Music Festival or the Beethovenists, 1838), and the sculptor Max Klinger, even as late as 1900, could see in him the divine superman, the romantic magician; while Hanslick in *The Beautiful in Music* (1854) and Pfitzner, as late as 1919 in his *Neue Ästhetik* (New Esthetic), regarded him as the master of the Classic form, the absolute musician unsicklied by any "poetical ideas." "In Beethoven classicism became romantic"; [44] how the understanding of Beethoven wavered under the influence of the Romantic concept of music and how it is exactly the interpretation of Beethoven that demonstrates the unity and indivisibility of the Classic-Romantic period has been briefly and instructively set forth by Joseph Schmidt-Görg. [45]

Given these assumptions, the demarcation of a Romantic period apart from a Classic period commonly adopted in the writing of music history appears questionable; it certainly cannot claim to possess the full weight of a genuine periodic structuring. Ernst Bücken [46] still attempted to present Beethoven as a pure Classicist and repeatedly attributes to him a thoroughly "anti-Romantic" attitude, in opposition to which he then introduces the new beginning of a Romantic period with Hoffmann, Weber, Dussek, Schubert, and the rest. Alfred Einstein [47] inclines to overestimate the social-revolutionary in Beethoven's character and thus to draw him into the neo-Romantic sphere; he expressly emphasizes that it was

44. Lang, *op. cit.*, p. 746. On this question, see also Jean Boyer, *Le "romantisme" de Beethoven,* Paris, 1938, and Jean Chantavoine and Jean Gaudefroy-Demombynes, *Le romantisme dans la musique européenne,* Paris, 1955.
45. Cf. MGG, article *Beethoven,* 1545–51.
46. Bücken, *op. cit.*
47. Einstein, *op. cit.*

Beethoven who set the pattern for the Romantics. He consequently stays clear of all antinomy between Romantic and Classic, but in so doing leaves open the question of their relation to each other and of their delimitation. Jacques Handschin, too, upholds the contrast between the two: Beethoven is "on the whole Classic rather than Romantic" because to him the sonata form was "still something very much alive" whereas to the Romantics it was something "inherently foreign." [48] This observation, in itself correct enough, hardly provides an adequate foundation on which to build a system of periodization. Handschin also sees the many strands that link Beethoven with the Romantics. However, when he tries to escape the dilemma by ranking Beethoven as the "master of the Empire," he is not clearing up the problem but skirting it. "Empire"— like *"Biedermeier,"* which is occasionally used to classify other composers of the Romantic era—is a concept in general cultural history and also a style-concept in the plastic arts, but remains inapplicable to music. Nor did Handschin recognize that the Classic-Romantic period begins long before Beethoven, and that Beethoven occupies but one of the many intermediate positions in the continuing development of this antinomy.

In his fundamental delineation of the age Lang [49] treats the music of the early Classic period, together with that of the *galant* and *empfindsam* styles, as a preliminary stage, and restricts the Classic period proper to Haydn and Mozart; Beethoven is, however, placed not in contrast but in logical sequence to them, which correctly carries out the close connection, indeed, the unity of Classic and Romantic: "Romanticism should not be taken as the antithesis of classicism, nor was it a mere reaction to it, but rather a logical enhancement of certain elements which in classicism were inherent and active, but tamed and kept in equilibrium." Only the subjectivistic features, which had long been pushing toward the surface, now stand out more sharply. "It is only in their vehemence that we feel a direct opposition to classic measure. And thereby the stylistic relationship between classicism and romanti-

48. *Musikgeschichte,* Basel, 1948, p. 355.
49. *Op. cit.*

cism seems determined." The Romantic era did not create a new
style; it remodeled and developed the Classic style. "Romanticism
is no more mere lawlessness than classicism is sheer form and
order. Romanticism is not, then, an adversary of classicism." And
further, "in combining the deification of Goethe and Beethoven
with their own ideals, they [the Romantics] merely carried the ac-
complishment of classicism into the unrealizable." [50] Lang accordingly entitles the chapter in question "The Confluence of Classicism and Romanticism" and sees their further historic course as
drifting apart into the individual directions, personalities, and
countries involved in it.

Grout, too,[51] sees in Beethoven the connecting link between
the two tendencies and recognizes the unity of Classic and Romantic in him. Here appears the idea that through the sometimes thoroughly personal expression of his works Beethoven especially fired
the Romantic generation: "music as mode of self-expression."
"Romantic or not, Beethoven was the most powerful disruptive
force in the history of music. His works opened the gateway to a
new world." [52] Grout, too, sees in Haydn's *Creation* and *Seasons,*
in Mozart's *Don Giovanni* and *Magic Flute,* as in Beethoven's
Fifth and Ninth Symphonies, the deepest wellsprings of Romanticism,[53] and in later developments "a great variety of styles and
within its general unity . . . many contradictions and countercurrents"; for him, too, the music history of the 19th century resolves
into the multiplicity of tendencies and individual styles brought
about through personalities, compositional forms, and countries,
until "the late nineteenth and early twentieth centuries witnessed
the last stage of Romanticism and the transformation of the late-
Romantic idiom into a new musical language." [54]

Certain it is that musical historiography cannot do without the
concept of Romanticism. It is equally certain that this concept
alone cannot firmly define or delimit an epoch of music history.

50. *Ibid.,* p. 740.
51. Donald J. Grout, *A History of Western Music,* New York, 1960.
52. *Ibid.,* p. 491.
53. *Ibid.,* p. 499.
54. *Ibid.,* p. 568.

And it is absolutely certain that only in the fundamental unity of Classicism and Romanticism can be perceived the fundamental unity of the historical period that lasted from about the 1760s (if one includes its early stage) until the first decades of the 20th century. It is necessary to bear in mind that the beginnings of Romanticism were already contained in the beginnings of Classicism, were indeed to a great extent one with it; and it is equally necessary not to overlook the fact that the foundations of the Classic-Romantic style remained the same from the start to its final dissolution. Yet the differences in the music of the "Romantic age" are extraordinarily great: to describe the "style of musical Romanticism" would mean writing a music history of the 19th century.

IV

The Classic-Romantic Style in the 19th Century

Basically unchanged, then, the Classic canon of musical forms and elements, which we have exhaustively discussed above (pp. 30–74), also underlies the music of the Romantic era. It is impossible to describe its developments and modifications in all their detail, because they vary in so many ways from one composer to another, within the life-work of one and the same composer, from one country to another, and from one type of composition to another, and because in this process the canon itself gradually becomes worn and frayed, until finally the unifying model is lost. One can only sum up the basic features of this progression.

a] RHYTHM, METER, TEMPO

Periodicity of meter and refinement of rhythm remain fundamental from the first, though later with certain limitations. The principle of the eight-measure period holds even for Wagner and Strauss, although it is now extremely flexible and frequently overlaid by apparently free turns of invention, behind which the old schema often enough remains recognizable. Bruckner occasionally noted the number of measures in his periods in the margin of his scores; in Brahms, simple eight-measure periodicity often appears undisguised. The closer to the dance, the more uncomplicated: in Schubert's *German Dances,* the waltzes of Johann Strauss, and even Janáček's *Lachian Dances,* the metric organization is quite simple. It takes over in the song, too, and is only

later, with Hugo Wolf, Richard Strauss, Gustav Mahler, and others
(and, outside Germany, especially among the Czech composers),
altered to more complicated—yet hardly ever aperiodic—structures. Already in the High Classic such periodicity was often used
ad nauseam so that the more inventive composers refined, extended, abbreviated, veiled, or otherwise somehow enlivened it;
this happened increasingly in the 19th century, without the basic
scheme ever being altogether deserted. While Beethoven often
works with very daring overlappings, elisions, and the like, later
composers, quite to the contrary, much more frequently sought a
return to simplicity of periodic structure. Weber, Schubert, Schumann, Brahms, still more Mendelssohn, Joseph Joachim Raff, the
numerous virtuoso keyboard composers around Ignaz Moscheles
and Stephen Heller, the song composers around Mendelssohn and
Robert Franz, even Brahms not excepted, often use a surprisingly
simple periodicity, which in this special field may well relate to the
leaning toward folksong. But also in the symphony, the string
quartet, the sonata, etc., the situation is basically no different, even
though in details, of course, there is an enormous variety of devia-
tions.

Just as this fundamental structural principle, the eight-measure
period, can be seen to have undergone scarcely any further development during the course of the 19th century (indeed, by comparison with Beethoven, a retrogression rather), so also with rhythm,
which had in the Classic period been handled with the finest nu-
ance and sensibility, becoming an important element in conveying
expression. It is striking to note that the "Romantic" composers
often use it in stereotyped patterns. Rhythm is a weak side of
music in the Romantic era, and not only in the period of Impressionism,[55] regardless of whether one considers Impressionism to
be a late phase of the Classic-Romantic epoch or a special development *sui generis*. Schubert can write entire movements, especially ⁶⁄₈ finales, in one fixed rhythm; in other movements large sections are contrasted, each clinging to a constant rhythm. One

55. Cf. Hans Albrecht in MGG, article *Impressionismus,* especially
1076 ff.

recognizes Brahms, as well as Bruckner, by a characteristic use of rhythm—in itself often attractive as an appealing detail, but recurring frequently throughout their works—in which cross-rhythms and long, drawn-out syncopations play a part. The production of lesser composers—George Onslow, for example, Czerny, Adolf von Henselt, Albert Lortzing (but Spohr and Mendelssohn also not excepted), and in later decades Friedrich Gernsheim, Josef Rheinberger, Heinrich von Herzogenberg, Friedrich Kiel—often really do suffer from rhythmic monotony, which is one of the major reasons for their frequently being dull and tiresome. In the piano literature the tendency toward virtuosic brilliance (shared in one form or another by almost all compositions of the century) exerted a regularizing influence on rhythmic structures through its tinsel glitter; behind the elegant arabesques and traceries the rhythmic element is here often palpably neglected, a shortcoming that even Chopin and Liszt, among others, did not escape.

Rhythmic mobility was also hampered by the march-step (since Beethoven it had left lasting impressions in art music) and the stereotypes of waltz, galop, and other dance forms, as for example in Schumann. The compounding of complementary and conflicting rhythms (Schumann, Brahms); the mixture or superposition of binary and ternary rhythms (Brahms, Bruckner; good examples for study are the ensemble numbers in Verdi's *Falstaff*, a-Romantic though they may be in other respects); the shifting of accent in hemiolas and related structures; the whimsical interplay of rhythm and meter (Brahms); the emphasis on solemnly paced rhythms and their exaltation in hymn and chorale (Wagner, Bruckner); refined, highly pointed declamatory rhythm (Richard Strauss); the obscuring intensification of simple basic rhythms with quintuplets or septuplets or the like, beloved from early Chopin to Debussy and beyond; the frequent employment of written-out ritardandos or accelerandos; and, finally, the kaleidoscopic interchange of all these means and their sovereignly arbitrary use characterize especially the final stage of the process that buries the fine rhythmic sense of the Classic under a surfeit of alluring charms, not always successfully avoiding, however, the impression of a mechanical, harassed, stagnating activity.

For rhythm, too, it was the last works of Beethoven that provided the stimulus; in the *Missa solemnis* and the Ninth Symphony is prefigured everything the 19th century was able to develop in the realm of rhythm. With the accumulation of effects and their exaggerated use, the individual rhythmic motif often loses its power to make an impression. In any one of Bruckner's symphonies, for example, there is scarcely a single rhythmic motif that could not be exchanged for a similar one in another symphony. The rhythmic resources of the Viennese classics were exhausted by the end of the 19th century, and only when the national musics of the Eastern European peoples took shape did new rhythmic impulses grow out of them for European music. Mussorgsky, Dvořák, Smetana, Janáček, Bartók, and others unfolded new rhythmic forces from their native folk music.

With questions of tempo the situation is similar. That which resources of absolute speed could contribute to the originality of composition, Beethoven had already exhausted; in this respect his influence was highly "Romantic," because the Romantics again and again imitated his disposition of tempos and his tempo markings. The unusual slowness of his Largo and Adagio movements (which by mid-20th century were almost always taken much too fast), the bewitching (as even Goethe felt it) *prestissimo* of his scherzos and the strettos in his finales, the *ritmo di tre battuti* in the Ninth Symphony, *di quattro battuti* in the C-sharp minor Quartet, Op. 131; also his individually characterizing tempo prescriptions—as "Assai sostenuto," "Mit andacht" (with reverence), "Andante molto cantabile e non troppo mosso" (in the *Missa solemnis*), or "Lento assai, contante e tranquillo," "Grave, ma non troppo tratto" (not too dragging, in the Quartet in F, Op. 135); together with the extraordinary wealth of finely graded indications like "Adagio assai," "Adagio, ma non troppo," "Allegro vivace," "Allegro con spirito," "Allegro maestoso," "Allegro moderato," "Allegretto un poco," "Larghetto," and many others, in which Beethoven loved to convey exactly how he imagined the performance of his compositions—all these passed over into and through the 19th century and beyond, imitated again and again in countless variants and ramifications; there was nothing more to be developed out of them. Neither the most delirious passages in Richard Strauss's scores nor Bruckner's broadest hymn-movements could surpass Beethoven's tempos.

One cannot fail to observe a coarsening of tempos in the late Romantic period, and a sort of flight into extremes. Herewith the finer intermediate nuances gradually lost their effectiveness and tempo in the individual movement became less sensitive. Although along with Beethoven's methods the most exact possible fixing of tempo (upon occasion even by means of metronome markings) and with it the narrow restriction of the interpreter by painfully minute and strict prescriptions had been carried over into the Romantic period, the tendency toward extreme tempos and the relative neglect of the more intermediary ones leads to the paradoxical consequence that in performance the choice of tempo may vary widely without noticeably weakening the effect of the movement in question, so that in fact the interpreter's freedom is increased rather than lessened. No small part of the differences among the interpretations of modern conductors rests upon this empirical fact. How markedly this is a characteristic of the 19th century (since Beethoven) can be immediately and sensitively perceived if one imagines the same freedom of interpretation applied to music of the High Classic period.

b] Harmony and Tonality

The music of the Classic-Romantic era rests without qualification upon the major-minor system, the thorough chromaticization of which had in practice already taken place at the end of the Baroque era, while with the universal introduction of equal temperament nothing further stood in the way of unlimited enharmonic relations. If up to the end of Haydn and Mozart the minor tonalities had still been the exception with most composers and "reserved for rarer spheres of expression," [56] with Beethoven this state of affairs suddenly changed. "Beethoven's C minor" became

56. Cf. *Classic Music*, p. 37.

an abstract concept in the Romantic era, and it was not by chance that Hoffmann's enthusiasm took fire from the Fifth Symphony. Outright symbol of the tragic, it finds its counterpart in "Beethoven's C major," symbol of the triumphal. In between lies the expressive range of tonalities, with its infinitely rich graduations, poetically described by Schubart and Hoffmann in such terms as: "A-flat minor: Ah, they bear me into the land of eternal longing . . . ; E major: They have handed me a glorious crown . . . ; A minor: Why flee from me, fair maiden?" and so forth.[57]

In practice, minor keys appear alongside major keys with equal rank and frequency, and the more remote among them, used but seldom and during the High Classic era only in passing, now achieve a preferential position. Beethoven's Quartet, Op. 131 without hesitation uses C♯ minor and G♯ minor for its string texture. With highly developed string technique and constantly improving wind-instrument mechanics, difficulties of intonation no longer play a role in the orchestra either. Piano music, as early as Field, Schubert, Chopin, and Heller, increasingly favors the remoter tonalities, which correspond with the Romantic need for the unusual and the fabulous, and furthermore lend piano tone a special brilliance. Beethoven had already written a piano sonata in F♯ (Op. 78), Weber a very brilliant one in A♭ (Op. 39), Hummel a *Grande Sonate* in F♯ minor (Op. 81), Schumann his famous Sonata in F minor (Op. 14). If wide possibilities in the selection and combination of tonalities still remained unexplored in the High Classic era, 19th-century musicians from now on make unlimited use of them, without any fundamental change taking place on this account in the composer's attitude toward tonality and without any serious threat to the basic major-minor system occurring up to the end of the era. Until Richard Strauss, Debussy, Janáček, *et al.,* every composition and every texture is set in a clearly definable major or minor tonality, however richly differentiated or broadly extended this tonality may be. Not until after 1910, with Bartók, Schoenberg, Stravinsky, and the rest, does one arrive at compositions that are no longer intended in the major-minor sense and can

57. Hoffmann, *Kreislers poetische-musikalischer Klub.*

no longer be so understood.

A characteristic of the Romantic treatment of tonalities is the fluid change, the imperceptible gliding of modulations and deceptive progressions. In the High Classic period, the cadence still corresponds to the articulation of the movement and has constructive value; it is the punctuation mark that makes logical connections clear. Modulations as a rule take place in connection with cadences and the joining of sections; they, too, have a constructive value. They place different tonal regions side by side or in opposition and lend plasticity to the movement's course. Deceptive progressions are used as a means of expression to convey passing nuances, to darken, to clarify, for changes of mood, and so forth. In this respect Beethoven in his early and middle periods is thoroughly a "Classic"; cadences and modulations in the main coincide with the structural organization, and passing deceptive progressions are moreover not frequent with him.

Key relationships between the movements of cyclical works also for the most part remain faithful to the Classic order with Beethoven; outer movements of sonatas, string quartets, symphonies, concertos, and so forth, are set in the basic tonality or its parallel, middle movements in closely related keys. Exceptions already occur in Haydn, and in Beethoven's middle works they become more numerous (for example, in the Triple Concerto, Op. 56: C–Ab–C; the Piano Concerto No. 5, Op. 73: Eb–B–Eb; the Piano Trio, Op. 97: Bb–D–Bb; the Piano Sonata, Op. 101: A–F–a–A; Op. 106: Bb–f♯–F–Bb), and the last string quartets arrive at very surprising key relationships. But these remain exceptions. Schubert and Weber, Spohr and Mendelssohn, even Schumann and Brahms handle their tonalities quite conventionally, and this is true in the relationship between the movements of cyclical works as well as in the sections within a movement; it is unusual when Brahms, say, in his First Symphony, Op. 68, sets the four movements in c–E–Ab–c, or when Bruckner, who otherwise clings strictly to closely related keys, in his last symphony (in which the first movement and the scherzo have been in D minor) sets the Trio in B and the Adagio in E. Similarly with Dvořák,

Grieg, and others. Even in Berlioz, series of closely related tonalities predominate. Those key-sequences that seem unusual by comparison with the High Classic (as in the above examples) are almost always based on the fact that, after Beethoven, keys related by a third had come to be felt as closely connected, as valid as dominant, subdominant, and parallel relationships. Much of the effectiveness of tonal contrast in 19th-century compositions rests on this relationship of the effectiveness of modulation beginning with Schubert (whose own frequent deceptive harmonic shifts and evasions occur as a rule between third-related keys). Only at the very end of the century, with Debussy and Strauss, is a perfectly free treatment of tonalities arrived at, no longer adhering to any conventional rules.

Over and above this, harmony in the Romantic era is marked by the luxuriant use of alterations through which it acquires its character of supple gliding, of fluid transitions that veil its contours; it is often difficult to distinguish between deception and modulation. Harmonic alteration reaches a peak in Wagner's *"Tristan* chord," a much-cited standard example, and it became one of the prerequisites for the shifting harmony of Impressionism before the novel nature of which "the romantic concept breaks down." [58] The quality of modulation is furthermore enriched through extensive use of chromatic and enharmonic possibilities, which with Schumann and Brahms, and still more with Wagner and Strauss, reach their limits. From this point the dissolution of the Classic-Romantic tonal orders ultimately follows. Open octaves, fifths, and fourths; parallel-chord progressions (Debussy); unprepared and unresolved dissonances; fourth-chords (Scriabin); the piling-up of augmented and diminished intervals; tiers of thirds; accumulated substitution of seventh-, ninth-, and eleventh-chords for triads and their inversions; added-sixth chords, etc., etc.—these are the stimulants that in ever-increasing measure loosen the structural solidity of composition, undermine the feeling for the logic of construction, and finally lead to the limit of what can still be achieved and understood within the major-minor system without losing the basic

58. Hans Albrecht, *op. cit.,* especially 1051.

sense of tonality. Strauss, Reger, Janáček, and many others occasionally give up real modulation entirely, setting key rigidly beside key; the statement "Any chord can be followed by any other" comes from Max Reger's letter of July 17, 1902, to C. Sander (Reger himself ascribes it to Liszt, which does not seem quite credible).

Add to all this the piling of one key upon another (Strauss, Debussy, Reger) by which a sort of "polytonality" may be achieved, and the moment has come when keys, chords, and modulations can no longer be considered as such, or as constructive values, but only as color effects. The process of blending tonal and coloristic values that had, like so many others, begun with Beethoven[59] is at an end, even though the possibilities latent in the Classic-Romantic system have not been altogether exhausted. Leoš Janáček is one of the composers who at the very end of the period were still extracting altogether novel combinations out of that system, thus still adhering to it, while Schoenberg, Webern, and Stravinsky had already arrived at "atonal" procedures. But the major-minor system and the laws of harmonic progression were never forcibly broken during the Classic-Romantic period, only very much relaxed, manifestly enriched, given fluidity, right up to the brink of their dissolution. "Composers . . . from Bach to Fauré have had certain common habits in forming sequences of chords. If the music of Bach and that of Fauré do not sound alike, it is not because their basic chordal progressions differ essentially; they differ only superficially in that the individual chords of the latter may be more complicated and colored.[60]

c] Motif, Theme, and Thematic Work

The supremacy of melody over all other elements, which was the first rule in the early and High Classic period, remained in effect in the later phases of the Classic-Romantic era

59. Cf. *Classic Music*, p. 45.
60. Willi Apel, *Harvard Dictionary of Music*, Cambridge, Mass., 1944, p. 317; also cf. for the functionless apposition of chords, Albrecht in MGG, article *Instrumentation*, 1269 ff.
61. Cf. *Classic Music*, pp. 45–55.

and was, indeed, amply confirmed. Innumerable statements by composers, from Beethoven to Strauss, give us to understand that they took special trouble in the unfolding of melody, whereas much less is said about harmony and tonality. If harmony as an esthetic problem was still a lively concern of the first Romantic generation—Anton Reicha at one point speaks of "the finer combinations of harmony" as "reflections from the unconscious" [62]—it seems to us that to those who came later it was rather a matter of craftsmanship than of esthetic speculation. To this the greatly increasing number of harmony textbooks in the 19th century bears witness. Questions of melodic construction, on the other hand, from both technical and esthetic points of view, form matter for debate among composers. Reicha published a *Traité de la mélodie* in 1814 and textbooks on composition often devote long chapters to questions of melody, as do Heinrich Christoph Koch's *Versuch einer Anleitung zur Komposition* (1782–93), Johann Bernhard Logier's *System der Musikwissenschaft und der musikalischen Komposition* (1827), Adolf Bernhard Marx's *Die Lehre von der musikalischen Komposition* (1837–47), and especially Hugo Riemann's revised edition of the same work under the title *Grosse Kompositions-Lehre* (1902), Ludwig Bussler's *Elementarmelodik* (1879), and Salomon Jadassohn's *Das Wesen der Melodie in der Tonkunst* (1899).

In any case, melody became in practice more and more the element that most spontaneously expressed the originality of the composer at the same time providing the subject for hard work. Richard Strauss told how in his Meiningen days Brahms advised him to "Look carefully at the Schubert dances and test yourself in the invention of simple and eight-measure melodies," [63] and most revealingly remarked in a conversation with the music critic Max Marschalk: "I work a long time on melodies; it is a long way from the first inspiration to the final shaping of a melody. . . . Everything is taught in the conservatories, excepting only the construction of melodies. . . . The motif is a matter of spontaneous im-

---

62. According to Bücken, *op. cit.*, p. 25.
63. Trenner, *op. cit.*, p. 34.

pulse; it is the inspiration, and most people are satisfied with the inspiration, whereas it is its development that first reveals true art" (here follow examples from Meyerbeer, Mozart, Beethoven, and statements about his own building of melodies). "A melody that seems to be born of the moment is almost always the result of hard work." [64]

That these remarks apply to countless Romantic composers is obvious; the "inspiration" that Strauss identifies with the motif is laboriously developed into a melody—Beethoven's sketchbooks are early testimony; Haydn, too, once expressed himself similarly in talks with Michael Kelly—and this effort is often noticeable in Romantic melody. The spinning out of such melodies is closely connected with the inclination of the age toward periodicity and the building of long, compound periods. This may explain two points that strike us in Romantic music: on the one hand, a preference for arching melodic lines that begin hesitantly, unfolding slowly, over and over, and only in their further course swinging wide and stretching into periods of many sections (Schubert, Brahms); and, on the other, the markedly songlike character of these melodies.

With Schubert, early in the 19th century, a full flowering of the art song had set in that lasted until the end of the period, and Schubert was one of the most gifted and fruitful inventors of melody in the whole history of music. Nineteenth-century instrumental melody was profoundly influenced by him and by the ubiquitous genus of the song—so deeply, indeed, that the difference between instrumental theme and song melody, which was still decisively significant for Beethoven, is further and further wiped out. Innumerable instrumental themes could be sung to appropriate texts (and were so sung), and from Schubert to Brahms, Liszt, and Dvořák song melodies were countless times used as "themes" for instrumental compositions. In most of Schubert's instrumental works the "themes" are nothing but long-spun song melodies—for example, the Cello Quintet in C (D. 956), the B minor Symphony (D. 759), the B♭ Piano Sonata (D. 960)—hence they are much rather related to the thematic material of Mozart's late works than to the

64. *Ibid.*, pp. 79–81.

abrupt, aphoristic themes, confined to brief energy-laden units, of late Beethoven. This song-melody type of theme invaded the instrumental compositions of the entire Romantic period; it is found in Mendelssohn as well as in Brahms and Schubert; is valid for Weber, Spohr, and the many smaller masters; governs the smallest lyric piano pieces as well as the symphony, string quartet, and solo concerto. To it the instrumental music of the 19th century owes its emphatically lyric character and hence its worldwide success.

One cannot fail to see, on the other hand, that this is a consequence of the decay of formal construction, a sort of *fin de siècle* phenomenon. As a result of the delight in melody that characterized Romantic instrumental music, the original meaning of sonata form—the struggle of opposites and their conflict in the developing elaboration of the initial thematic material—dissolves into the highly expressive but formally weak opposition of areas of feeling and of tonal planes. Beethoven's drama, stirring, passionate, turns into Schubert's elegiac, reflective idyll. "Thematic logic is the *sine qua non* of sonata construction, and requires specifically symphonic material. This fundamental requirement the romantic sonata lacked." [65] So it comes about that with Schubert and Schumann, even with Brahms, and quite particularly with many composers less able at architectonics, constructive interest in form as such, and in the thematic work from which it is built recedes into the background, form often appearing to be merely a shelter for the unfolding of melody, for harmonic and rhythmic excitement, and for the colorfulness of instrumental sound, while the thematic work of the Classic period dies away to eventual extinction.

It was one of the greatest achievements of the so-called "neo-German" movement to have opened a new path in this regard. In Wagner, Bruckner, and Richard Strauss a new spirit of thematic invention appeared that again set free stronger formative powers. Bruckner's symphonies link up anew with Beethoven's thematic technique, working with brisk, energy-laden motifs each of which is developed within itself, fully exploited, contrasted, combined, counterpointed with others; out of this motivic work grows an ex-

65. Lang, *op. cit.,* p. 818.

tensive thematic complex that in itself forms a tense and firm symphonic unit. Such complexes are then handled in larger dimensions in a manner similar to that used for the opening thematic material; thus it is that Bruckner achieves the grandiose towering waves of intensification so characteristic of him. The whole is at the same time linked together by important cadential structures; in his first symphonies *Generalpausen* originally stood between the sections. In his outer movements, even in his slow movements, Bruckner avoids the spinning of motifs into song-melody periods, thus escaping the danger of bogging down in lyricism. In this sense he may be called the only genuine symphonist since Beethoven.

Wagner transferred the same basic principles to opera. His "leitmotifs" are very close to the opening material of Bruckner's symphonies and give rise in a comparable manner to symphonic textures quite independent of their programmatic function and of operatic action. Pieces like the *Ride of the Valkyries,* for example, or the *Magic Fire Music* from *Walküre* are in their motivic invention and symphonic elaboration the exact opposite of Verdi's or Meyerbeer's operatic lyricism and rank rather with Bruckner's developmental groups. One should of course not overlook the fact that Schubert's complexes of songlike themes also provide a starting point for the complex theme-groups of Wagner and Bruckner. The three-part layout of the theme group in the Adagio of Bruckner's Fifth Symphony (also that of his Eighth) and its development into the five-part layout of the whole movement may well, despite the contrast between his technique of evolving motifs and Schubert's of spinning melody, trace back to the latter's own complex thematic layouts—as, for example, in the Cello Quintet (D. 956), the G major String Quartet (D. 887), the B minor and C major Symphonies (D. 759 and 944).

The formal basis for melodic structure was established by the Classic era, and its periodic construction [66] also underlies melody in the Romantic era. Analyses of the enormous treasure of melodies piled up by composers from Schubert to Brahms (and, of course, far beyond) yield in principle always the same schemata, although

66. See *Classic Music,* p. 49 ff.

the individual character and flow of the melodies is infinitely varied. Attempts to generalize concerning preferences in the Romantic era for rising or falling melodic lines, for small or large intervals, triadic or stepwise progression and the like are bound to remain unprofitable because it was exactly in the area of melody that the demand for originality allowed for the greatest freedom. With all caution, one may perhaps conclude that there is an inclination among Romantic composers toward integrated shaping of the melodic matter within itself, in that the general flow absorbs the motif as building material, rendering it unrecognizable as a separate building block (for example, the first themes of the first movements of Schubert's B minor and Mozart's G minor Symphonies), as well as a tendency toward stronger integration of melody with harmony. In all melodic writing of the Classic-Romantic period, indeed, melody and harmony are more or less integrated. Yet in the days of Schultz, Reichardt, Zelter, and in Haydn (but only partially in Mozart) one can imagine melodic invention as independent, without harmony: ". . . invention of a pretty melody is the work of one's own genius," said Haydn to Michael Kelly, "and such a melody needs no further embellishment in order to please; if you want to know whether it is really beautiful, sing it without accompaniment." [67] From Beethoven on, however, such integration increases markedly: the melody of the second movement of Beethoven's F minor Piano Sonata, Op. 57, for example, or of Brahms's F minor Piano Quintet, Op. 34 could hardly stand up, or would at least lose much of their charm, without the harmony that belongs to them.

Melody remains relatively most independent in the lied with piano; many strophic song melodies of Schubert, Schumann, Mendelssohn, Franz, *et al.* can be understood without their accompaniments. In this the orientation toward folksong and folk ballad is at work. In Romantic instrumental music, however, melody and harmony for the most part so closely interpenetrate that melodic invention forfeits its character, even essential elements of its conformation, when separated from its harmonic accompaniment.

67. Quoted from E. F. Schmid, *Joseph Haydn*, Kassel, 1934, p. 295.

This latter fact is of importance in instrumental music because the increasing integration of melody and harmony proves to be a hindrance on the path to thematic work. Developmental treatment of motivic material presupposes its adaptability, its mutability, its freedom from harmonic ties. It is significant that in Romantic instrumental music melodic ideas are repeated mostly with an unaltered, or only slightly altered, harmonic structure. In this field, too, the "new German" movement with Wagner and Bruckner first brought about a change; the motifs of both these composers are most readily transformable and can in the genuine sense be "developed." On this rest Wagner's "unending melody" and his capacity for unfolding broadly conceived orchestral textures as well as Bruckner's power in contrapuntal symphonic composition and in continuous development of his initial material in great waves of intensity.

d] Genres and Forms

The unity of Classic and Romantic is also borne out by the fact that their genres and forms are common to both and subject only to amplification, specialization, modification, and the like. None of the genres used in the High Classic period were given up by the Romantics, with the possible exception of the serenade, which occurs only occasionally—among the compositions of Beethoven, Brahms, Tchaikovsky, Hugo Wolf, Richard Strauss, Dvořák, Reger, and a number of lesser masters.[68] New to the instrumental repertory there appear only the fashionable and gradually stylized dance-types like the German dance, the *Schottisch* (écossaise), the waltz, polka, mazurka, galop, cancan, and so forth. The circumspection observed in the early and High Classic periods regarding the dance was no longer present among Romantic composers, dances taking more and more share in serious music.

This is true not only in the sense that, from Beethoven on, countless masters wrote dances in simple or in stylized forms—Beethoven's écossaises, Schubert's German dances, Chopin's mazurkas and waltzes, Weber's polonaises, Liszt's brilliant waltzes,

68. Cf. Hans Engel in MGG, article *Divertimento*.

czardas, and galops, the waltzes of Lanner and the two Strausses, the saucy cancans of Offenbach, etc., all the way to Brahms's *Liebeslieder Waltzes,* Opp. 52a and 65a, his Hungarian Dances, Dvořák's dumkas, furiants, Scottish Dances, Op. 41, and Slavonic Dances, Opp. 46 and 72, and so forth—but even more in the sense that dance forms and dance rhythms in general had extensively invaded instrumental art music, from the ländler-like trios in Schubert's sonatas and quartets to the dancelike motion that breaks through in the innumerable lyric piano pieces of Mendelssohn, Heller, Schumann, Moscheles, Brahms, Dvořák, etc., and stamps many movements of cyclical works. There are, at least in the realm of German Romanticism, but few composers like Wagner and Bruckner, who have not more or less richly paid tribute to the dance, while at the end of the period the waltz underwent a sort of apotheosis in Richard Strauss's *Rosenkavalier* (and a sort of persiflage in Ravel's *La Valse*). It is hardly necessary to mention that operetta and entertainment music live upon dances of all sorts. Since Beethoven, on the other hand, the scherzo in cyclical works by and large freed itself from the dance out of which it sprang, either turning to the Beethovenesque type of wildly agitated witch's ride (as in Bruckner especially) or using more leisurely and reflective types (as in Brahms's intermezzi) or, again being replaced by new dance-types (the dumkas and furiants of Dvořák).

A speciality of the 19th century is the lyric piece for piano, more rarely for other instruments or chamber ensembles, that gradually emerged through the development of the minuet into the *Charakterstück* (characteristic piece) of Beethoven, Schubert, Tomášek, Voříšek, and others and now appears under the most varied names—bagatelle, impromptu, intermezzo, elegy, eclogue, humoresque, nocturne, moment musical, barcarole, rhapsody, ballade, dithyramb, and the rest.[69] Mendelssohn's inspired title *Songs Without Words* clearly points to a second line of descent; these little works of art, which may well be counted among the most precious in all of Romantic music, grew out of the dance and the

69. Cf. the respective articles in MGG.

song, and they prove beyond the shadow of a doubt that the best, or at least one the best, accomplishments of the century lay in this field of small forms. From Schubert to Grieg, Gade, Reger, Mussorgsky, Dvořák, Janáček, and hundreds of others, such delicate or passionate mood-pictures or heartfelt outpourings were produced in abundance. Like the dances, they made their particular contribution to the cultivation of music in the middle-class home and to music education; for to the extent that art music destined for concert performance took on virtuoso character and exceeded the capacities of the dilettante (this process, too, really began with Beethoven), the lyric piano piece, together with the dance and the song, stepped into the breach, remaining well into the 20th century a favorite field of the cultured amateur and the music teacher.

Its chief competitor was the more brilliant entertainment music that since Chopin, Heller, Liszt, Thalberg, Henri Herz, Franz Hünten, and others had grown into an extensive literature and was often merged with the lyric piano piece—as in Mendelssohn, Moscheles, Schumann, and Brahms. This glittering bravura type of piece, however, falling prey to superficial tinkling effects, finally led to salon music and the degeneration of the whole genre. Schumann and his circle foresaw what was happening and violently attacked it in their writings and reviews. These types of composition never evolved distinctive forms of their own; on the contrary, interest in form remained quite in the background in comparison with the brilliance of technique and depth of emotional expression, so that for the most part the simplest song or rondo form covered the need. Tomášek, for example, in his Rhapsodies, like Schubert in his Impromptus, composed only a main first section and a middle section, simply repeating the first.

This whole "diminutive" art, perhaps the finest and most characteristic flower of Romanticism, deserves comprehensive study on its own account. In such a study the Romantic etude too, the concert etude (also called caprice, study, and the like) would take an honored place. For it not only had brilliant representation on the piano by Anton Reicha, Johann Baptist Cramer, Muzio Clementi, later by Ludwig Berger, Ignaz Moscheles, Kalkbrenner, Chopin,

Stephen Heller, Adolf von Henselt, Henri Bertini, Anton Rubinstein, and in Schumann's *Studies on the Caprices of Paganini,*
Opp. 3 and 10 (1832–33), and his *Symphonic Etudes,* Op.
13 (1834), Liszt's *Bravura Studies after Paganini's Caprices*
(1838), Brahm's *Variations on a Theme of Paganini,* Op. 35
(1862–63), and works by innumerable other composers even in
the 20th century; but also in countless cases it left testimony to a
high standard of cultural taste that accompanied the widespread interest in digital dexterity. It had its parallels in the realm of violin
music in Pierre Rode, Rodolphe Kreutzer, Niccolò Paganini, de
Bériot, Jacques-Féréol Mazas, Arnaud Dancla, and others, and in
cello music in Friedrich Dotzauer, Friedrich Grützmacher, and
the rest, as well as in other instrumental fields. And here, too, belong, finally, such much-beloved virtuoso compositions as the concert fantasy, the bravura fantasy, and the like, that found their
most prominent exponent in Liszt. It is especially in this wide field
of "diminutive" art, beside that of orchestral music, that the problem of program music came to the fore (see below). Many compositions of this sort (by Mendelssohn and Schumann, Mussorgsky
and Scriabin, Grieg and Gade, Dvořák and Janáček, and so on)
bear programmatic titles, thus winning a place for themselves in
the favorite repertory of the nonprofessional player and helping to
keep alive the never-yet-settled argument over "programmatic"
and "absolute" music.

Among the older instrumental genres that continued to be extensively cultivated in the 19th century belongs the variation cycle,
now adopted in all sorts of instrumental music—solo, ensemble,
orchestral—in music for piano or harp as in that for piano trio
and string quartet, in the sonata as in the symphony. Here the
Classic model [70] was fairly soon overpowered by the new impulses, purposes, and effects. Beethoven produced one of the new
models. In his *Righini Variations* of 1794 he burst through the
hitherto prevailing limits of figuration and with the help of virtuosic skill subjected the theme to formal alteration and at the
same time to fresh contextual interpretation; in the F major Varia-

70. Cf. *Classic Music,* p. 55 ff.

tions, Op. 34 (1802), he broke the bonds of uniform tonality and harmonic substructure, and made of each separate variation a lyric character-piece. His Thirty-two Variations in C minor for piano (1806), the *Diabelli Variations,* Op. 120 (1819–23), the variations in his last Piano Sonata, Op. 111 (1821–22), in the Piano Trio, Op. 97 (1811), in the C♯ minor String Quartet, Op. 131 (1826), in the "Eroica" Symphony, Op. 55 (1804), elevate this genre of composition from its former purpose of half improvised entertainment, half virtuoso showpiece, into the most exalted regions of artistic expressiveness. In this field of the variation Beethoven's influence was truly revolutionizing: he freed the form from the fetters of a conventional, although highly spiritualized sort of musical diversion (Mozart, Haydn) and stamped it with the gravity of high art.

A second new impulse came from the Romantic revival of Bach's *Goldberg Variations;* Hoffmann discovered in them a mine of "poetic ideas." [71] Later on they made a deep impression on Schumann and Brahms; into the 19th-century art of variation writing, the *Goldbergs* introduced the contrapuntal canonic element, as well as the idea of adapting individual variations to other familiar types of composition, and probably also—through the concluding variation with its use of merry folk tunes—the witty or parodistic feature we meet in so many sets of variations up to Reger's *Telemann* and *Hiller Variations.*

A third new impulse came from the brilliant piano music of composer-pianists like Nikolaus Joseph Hüllmandel, Kalkbrenner, Steibelt (to whom Beethoven played his *Righini Variations*), pushing into the foreground of the piano variation the virtuoso element already noticeable in Beethoven, that with Schubert and Weber often approaches the brilliant salon-variation and later, with Liszt and others brings the variation-cycle down to the level of the potpourri and the transcription. Czerny brought out a *Systematic Introduction to Improvisation* in 1836, dealing with the brilliant

71. The original edition of 1742 was presumably not easily accessible; copies had been circulated and a new edition seems to have appeared in Vienna or Zurich around 1802.

variation, the bravura fantasy, and the potpourri; in 1837 Liszt, jointly with Thalberg, Johann Peter Pixis, Herz, Czerny, and Chopin, published—under the title of *Hexaméron*—a variation-cycle on the march from Bellini's *I Puritani.*

Throughout the 19th century all these types of variation were pursued, partly following different aims and tendencies, partly blended in manifold ways and used in compositions of every sort; their number is enormous. Sometimes they came out as independent works, sometimes (perhaps even more often) within the framework of larger cyclical works.

The orchestral variation as an independent work, as we know it in Brahms's *Variations on a Theme of Haydn,* Op. 56a (1873) or Reger's *Hiller Variations,* Op. 100 (1907), is comparatively rare; in this category belong Dvořák's *Symphonic Variations,* Op. 78 (1877), César Franck's *Variations symphoniques* for piano and orchestra (1885), Sir Hubert Parry's *Symphonic Variations* (1897), Richard Strauss's *Don Quixote* (1897), Sir Edward Elgar's *Enigma Variations* (1899), and others. In symphonies, symphonic poems, chamber-music works, and sonatas of every conceivable sort, from Schubert's "Death and the Maiden" String Quartet in D minor (D. 810; 1824–26) to Dvořák's A minor String Sextet, Op. 48 (1878) and way beyond, there lies hidden an abundance of variation-cycles, "miniature art" in their own way, that belong to the finest fruits of 19th-century music.

Among old traditional types of composition the concerto for solo instrument with orchestra also flourished exuberantly during the 19th century—the virtuoso element in particular, as in other genres, now moving into the foreground. Here, too, Beethoven's concertos led the way, combining as they did the most original inventive fantasy with vigorous form and highly exacting technical brilliance. The Concertos in G, Op. 58, (1805–06) and E♭, Op. 73 (1809) indisputably mark the high point of the Romantic piano concerto, just as the Concerto in D, Op. 61 (1806) became the definitive model for the Romantic violin concerto. The advanced violin technique of Gaviniès and Viotti, and the keyboard brilliance of Hüllmandel and Steibelt were here raised to spiritual grandeur by seriousness of content and strength of form. All through this period Beethoven's type of symphonic concerto, which draws the solo instrument more or less into the thematic work and the formal construction, competed with the more brilliant bravura concerto, which gives precedence to the soloist and keeps the orchestra busy with preludes and interludes and with accompaniment. In the period from Dussek, Berger, Field, Moscheles, Kalkbrenner, Herz, Weber, Chopin, Mendelssohn, and so many others, to Liszt, Brahms, Lalo, Saint-Saëns, Rubinstein, Tchaikovsky, Reger, and—for the violin—Spohr, Bruch, Mendelssohn, Brahms, Tchaikovsky, Dvořák, Pfitzner, and all the rest, the number of solo concertos is legion.[72] Of the symphonie concertante, a genre so popular and widespread in Mozart's Mannheim-Paris period, we find on the contrary but few examples in the 19th century; works like Beethoven's Triple Concerto in C for piano, violin, and cello, Op. 56 (1803–04) or Brahms's Double Concerto in A minor for violin and cello, Op. 102 (1887) are rather isolated examples, though this special type is occasionally represented here and there among the concertos of other composers. The foundation remains the Classic three-movement form, with a first movement built on mingled sonata and concerto elements, a lyric, mostly songlike middle movement, and a rondo- or sonata-like finale; sometimes—not often—a scherzo or a transitional movement appears before the finale, but technical forms foreign to the concerto, such as the variation, for example, are rarely used.

The sonata remained the basic and generally valid large form in the 19th century too, in its manifold settings: for piano alone, for one string or wind instrument with piano, much less often for string or wind duo or trio without piano, for all varieties of chamber ensemble—piano trio (since in the Classic period, the string trio remains rare), string quartet, quintet, sextet, and finally the orchestral symphony. In contrast to the Classic period, four movements have now become the rule: an opening sonata movement is followed by a slow songlike movement and a scherzo (often in the

72. Cf. Hans Engel in MGG, article *Das Konzert*, section C: *Das Instrumental-Konzert*.

opposite order), and for the most part the finale again consists of
a sonata movement, rather looser in form, the rondo seeming, generally speaking, to have become more rare; where it does occur,
mostly in the piano sonata, it appears as "rondo brillant." A set of
variations may also take the place of the slow movement or the
finale, more rarely of the first movement.

The forms of the separate movements undergo a great many
changes. In the first movement, still quite frequently ushered in by
a slow introduction in the manner of Haydn (Beethoven's First
Symphony in C, Op. 21, and Seventh in A, Op. 92; Schubert's C
major Symphony, D. 944; Brahms's Symphony in C minor, Op.
68, etc.), the bithematicism customary since Beethoven's early
piano sonatas is considered the rule. However, the closing theme
of the Classical exposition rapidly gains importance, and in Schubert's late piano sonatas and chamber-music works already seems,
now and then, very like a third theme. As the themes themselves
incline to broaden out in groups (see p. 144), an exposition often
results in which the distinction between genuine thematic constitu-
ents and transitional accessory sections is lost and instead the
grouping falls into three large contrasting complexes of practically
equal value and weight (as in Schubert's Cello Quintet in C, D.
956, or Brahms's Fourth Symphony in E minor, Op. 98). This
structure took on great significance in Bruckner's symphonies and
is the rule with him. The broad development of songlike themes
seldom accords, however, with an equivalent developmental elaboration (see p. 143). Here the path of most of the Romantics leads
away from Beethoven, whom Bruckner was the first to follow
again to the full (see pp. 143 f. and 158). Most composers are content to replace thematic development by filling in the middle section
of the movement with new, inventive modulations, with extensive
and brilliant figuration, or with melodic and harmonic spinning-out
of the opening material (Schubert, Schumann, Mendelssohn, Spohr,
and Brahms do these things), more or less abandoning genuine
thematic work. The first movement of Schumann's B♭ Symphony,
Op. 38, gives the effect of a three-part song form of very broad dimensions, and the same holds true of many Romantic symphonies.

Into the piano sonata (and often also into the first movements of symphonies and chamber works) virtuoso passages find their way, elements from other types of composition. In the piano sonata especially, we find such elements from the lyric piano piece, episodic inventions, and the like (as with Brahms), which contribute to sound and content with fantasy and feeling but weaken the formal structure; only in the hands of such an unusually stern formalist as Bruckner do they contribute simultaneously to enriching the content and strengthening the construction. Still other disintegrative tendencies join in. Often now the movement does not begin, as in Beethoven, with the theme strongly outlined; rather, it evolves from some rhythmic or melodic introductory figuration, out of which the theme only slowly emerges or becomes recognizable. Very characteristic in this respect are the beginnings of Schubert's B minor Symphony (D. 759) and String Quartet in G (D. 887). The former opens with a songlike theme in the basses, joined by an undulant figure in the upper strings and only as this continuous motion proceeds does the theme blossom forth in oboe and clarinet. In the string quartet, something entirely new takes place: a dynamic crescendo and an oscillation between G major and G minor become constitutive elements out of the spasmodic beginnings of which the theme grows. Major-minor fluctuations play a very large role throughout the Romantic era (this whole Schubert quartet lives on them), serving to conceal schematic tonal substructures and to bring about fluctuating excitements. Composers similarly like to conceal joints in the construction through gently fluent transitions; the quite imperceptible entry of the reprise in the first movement of the same Schubert quartet is an example, for which the pattern had been set in Beethoven's "Eroica." Brahms, in his First Symphony, Bruckner very frequently, and countless others made use of this device.

In this category also belongs the fading-out or sudden breaking-off of a movement, which is already occasionally employed by Beethoven as a surprise ending (first movement of the Eighth Symphony, F major, Op. 93) and often used to leave the outcome of a movement in suspense, as with the characteristically abrupt endings beloved of Janáček. When most composers are not strongly purposeful about form, then form itself seems but an external housing for regions of expression and planes of color, and thus means of this sort cast an additional veil over the movement and lull the listener in the magic of their sensually harmonious sound, so that he is not provoked to any co-operative interest in the music—indeed, is not even permitted to share in it. A pleasurable intoxication takes the place of Goethe's "thinking enjoyment."

Herein perhaps lies one of the deepest contrasts between Classicism and Romanticism, since in the former the music itself demands energetic personal co-operation from the listener, whereas in the latter he is actually compelled to give himself over to a sweet passivity.[73] The Romantics were all inexhaustible in their invention of such shrouding sorcery through tonal, rhythmic, harmonic, and melodic means, and their music is the more romantic in effect the more they made use of them. Prescribed fluctuations in tempo, broadenings (Brahms's frequent "tranquillos"), accelerandos, delirious prestos at the close (since Beethoven), prescribed dynamic shadings, modulations brusque or smooth, mysterious whispering effects (Schumann's "Stimme aus der Ferne" in the eighth Novellette of Op. 21) combined with literary allusions—Berlioz's to Byron in *Harold in Italy,* Liszt's to Shakespeare in *Hamlet* and Schiller in *Die Ideale,* Schumann's to Hoffmann in *Kreisleriana* or to the *Marseillaise* in his sonata-like *Faschingsschwank aus Wien*—all stimulate the listener's imagination and somehow bring virtually every composition close to a "program" (however much its formal behavior may be that of a sonata or a symphony), thus forcing upon him a passive and receptive attitude, quite the opposite of that called forth by the music of the Classic era.

Things are similar with the other movements of sonata or symphony. Dimensions are even further enlarged than in first movements. The concise songlike, romance-like movements of the Classic composers expand, become multipartite, departing from the equable repose and restrained proportions that characterize them,

73. Cf. *Classic Music,* Ch. II.

despite their inner tension, in Mozart, even in his last works. This inner tension already begins to increase in Beethoven; it informs the Funeral March in the Third Symphony, the Hymn in the Ninth, and with these the model is established for the countless similar character pieces that constitute the slow movements of symphonies, string quartets, and sonatas in the Romantic period: for example, the "feierlich" transition to the Finale in Schumann's Third Symphony in E♭ major, Op. 97; the ballade-like Romanze in his Fourth, in D minor, Op. 120; the Andante moderato in Brahms's Fourth, in E minor, Op. 98, with its yearning melancholy that rises to an outburst of grief and then sinks back into itself again; the grandiose mounting hymnic layout of Bruckner's slow movements. All this may offer little new as concerns form in comparison with the Classic slow movement, yet there is a change in the psychic content: it now binds the listener in its spell and robs him of the freedom to "underlay these things with something of his own heart and soul," as Goethe put it.[74] It is in this connection that in Romantic symphonies, quartets, and sonatas, the slow movement not infrequently provides the center of gravity and the point of highest concentration in the whole cycle. The equilibrium is disturbed, "participation in the particular" (Goethe again) demands its rights.

In scherzos, too, the growth in dimensions is striking. As early as 1845–46, that of Schumann's Second Symphony in C, Op. 61, runs to almost 400 measures, while Bruckner's scherzos later reach lengths of over 500 measures. Many follow the Beethoven type (cf. p. 147 f.), not infrequently they still adhere to the Classic minuet scheme (Schubert), or they take the form of moderately fast idyllic and meditative character pieces (e.g. Schumann's Third Symphony), or give place to dance movements (as is often the case in Dvořák). There is a rich choice, and the tendency to the character piece is even clearer here than in the slow movements. Where the Beethoven type rules, it is not infrequently equipped with two trios (as it often is with Schumann). The trios themselves are always of strongly contrasting character and are frequently

74. To Eckermann, January 12, 1827.

written in strongly contrasting tonalities, rhythms, or meters. So modified, the scherzo movement moves out of the cyclic group in far greater degree than does the Classical symphony's minuet movement, raising its claim to be understood as separate piece *sui generis*.

The weak point in the Romantic construction of cyclic sonatas and symphonies often lies in the finale. While in Haydn and Mozart there is still no finale that does not round off the cycle in a natural and spontaneous manner, serenely reconciling all contrasts, the Romantic composer approaches the finale of his cycle with uncertainty. He is no longer concerned only with restoring the balance and arriving at the *lieto fine,* the happy ending; his mind is set instead on the build-up of a movement that will crown the whole cycle, making it rise to an exultant conclusion or tempering it down to a despondent resignation. The closing strettos in the symphonies and chamber-music works of Brahms and Dvořák are often martial and triumphant, bold and high-spirited; Tchaikovsky's Sixth Symphony in B minor closes in enigmatic dejection. With his Fifth Symphony, Beethoven had set the standard *per aspera ad astra,* and this was now varied in countless ways throughout the century. Among romantic composers the construction of such finales often seems artificial or studied, and the form that the Classic masters achieved with a turn of the hand (looser sonata form with inserts, regular sonata-rondos or the like, rarely variation-cycles as in Brahms's E♭ Clarinet Sonata, Op. 120, No. 2) does not always succeed in convincing. The major endings Schumann likes to append to his finales in minor sometimes seem affected, and the themes Schubert and Weber invent for theirs, not to mention those of Mendelssohn and Brahms, are often quite weak. The finale of Brahms's Fourth Symphony, the E minor, is a passacaglia on a chaconne bass from the cantata BWV 150, allegedly by Bach; for all its admirable wealth of invention it is not a satisfying finish to the cycle. Tchaikovsky's finale to his Fifth Symphony in E minor, Op. 64, is loud and theatrical and has a bombastic stretto. Spohr's Third Symphony in C minor closes with an affected and operatic finale. Dvořák and others are apt to take

refuge in the always effective world of folklore. Schubert's finales
are content with a poetic spinning out of regularly constructed conventional forms and through their excessive length (Symphony in C
major, D. 944: 1158 measures) betray the fact that here a basic
problem remains unsolved.

In this Bruckner is again an exception. In his finales he undertakes to gather up again in a powerful flood tide the material of
one or more of the preceding movements and through mounting
waves of symphonic texture—often by means of a contrapuntal
piling-up of theme on theme into which he introduces devotional
chorale-like interpolations—to totally exhaust the thematic content
of the cycle, achieving apotheoses in which the entire work is
swept into a final triumphant unity. The attempts of later composers linking up with Bruckner—e.g. Mahler—might at most out-
sound, but could not outdo him.

The means employed and the results achieved fluctuate considerably. In every regard Romantic subjectivism held its own roads
open. Yet it may be remarked, as a trait common to all cyclical
works produced in the Romantic period, that the Classical symphony and sonata, and especially those of Beethoven, remained before everyone's eyes as an ideal—never attainable but to be striven
toward ever anew. Wagner's well-known remark—that after Beethoven no more symphonies could be composed—contains a grain
of truth that holds for the whole century. All the Romantic era's
originality and all its power of invention, however delusive, however overwhelming to the senses, cannot disguise the fact that in
this field more was frequently intended than achieved, that constructive vigor had slackened and that symphonies, sonatas, string
quartets, etc. are often nothing more than ingenious or sensitively
conceived corollaries of small lyric forms. Without much effort one
could string together several separate lyric pearls from a Schubert
piano trio, a Brahms piano quartet, a Mendelssohn symphony; try
this with Beethoven or Bruckner, and the profound difference becomes evident.

Here, too, undoubtedly lies one of the roots of the Romantic
composers' dissatisfaction with themselves; they suffered from the

distance they must have recognized between the tasks imposed on them by a challenging tradition and their own talents, which they expended upon the flowering of Romantic lyricism. In letters and writings from Schubert on, they often enough called attention to this tormenting self-awareness.

Here, too, lies exposed the root, or at least one of the roots, from which there grew up in the 19th century that descriptive orchestral composition—whether dramatic or lyric, pictorial or contemplative—the symphonic poem (in the broadest sense of the term). The quantity of such compositions, from Berlioz's *Symphonie fantastique* ("An episode in the life of an artist"; 1830), *Harold en Italie* (1834), *Roméo et Juliette* (1839), Liszt's *Ce qu'on entend sur la montagne* (1849 ff.) and *Tasso* (1849) to those written by hundreds of composers (Mussorgsky, Tchaikovsky, Rimsky-Korsakov, Smetana, Dvořák, *et al.*), up to Strauss's *Tod und Verklärung* (1889), *Till Eulenspiegel* (1894–95), and *Ein Heldenleben* (1898), cannot by any means be fully surveyed; it embraces everything imaginable, from the delicacy of nature lyrics, through the pathos of historical painting, to the intimacy of psychological study. Here the unifying and cyclical restrictions of large form could be abandoned, and instead separate descriptive pieces could be freely strung together: here fantasy could do as it pleased. Inspiration, a sense of sonority and of effect, were more important than the convincing architectonics of large forms, and the composer could, according to his talents and his needs, lean upon literary subjects or the depiction of imaginary content, events, or characters.[75] It was a sort of outlet for an inner compulsion, as Berlioz and Liszt sometimes indicated in their writings; it was also an experiment in the capacity to mold form freely, to shape sound, unprejudiced by previous patterns. With occasional exceptions, many composers (like Schumann, Mendelssohn, Brahms, Bruckner, and Reger) disdained to use this outlet, preferring to exercise their powers again and again on the large forms, and often, in so doing, unintentionally impressed on their works a classicistic stamp.

75. Cf. Richard Strauss's letter to Romain Rolland cited above, fn. 28.

Basically, however, the symphonic poem, freely composed and unrestricted as to form, is a close relative of the small lyric character-piece and thus suited the Romantic composer's talents better than the symphony or the sonata. There is urgent need for a comprehensive study of this area, which until now has remained an almost inaccessible thicket in the history of Romantic music. Competition between symphony and symphonic poem in any case contributed much (especially after Debussy's impressionistic tone paintings had become universal models) to further dissolution of the convention of classical forms, causing the central core of tradition to fall away.

Though in the Romantic century instrumental music undoubtedly occupied the foreground of interest for both creator and consumer, a large amount of vocal music of all genres and tendencies was nevertheless composed. Taking the form, for the public music world, of church music, oratorio, opera, secular choral music, and song, and, for domestic music-making, primarily that of the song, its significance should by no means be underestimated. True, in the vocal field secular composition far outstripped religious in range and importance, but within the church music of both major denominations, creative life was anything but extinct. It is to be observed, however, that only a very small part of church-music composition can be subsumed under the catchword of "Romantic." By far the larger part is related to Romanticism only inasmuch as it sprang out of that period's own particular historicizing tendencies. Another and likewise not inconsiderable part, especially of Catholic music, was drawn from the a-Romantic, entirely classicistic arsenal of the Italian church music of Cimarosa, Ferdinando Paër, Joseph Rastrelli (to say nothing of the revival of older masters), whence the trend passed over to a large group of German composers, among them, for example, Johann Gottlieb Naumann, Franz Seydelmann, Josef Schuster, Adalbert Gyrowetz, et al.[76] Counterpart to this is the extensive church-music production of Germany and Austria, which, linking up with Mozart, Joseph Haydn, and

76. Cf. Otto Ursprung, *Katholische Kirchenmusik* Potsdam, 1931, p. 252 ff.

more especially his brother Michael, continued the Classical tradition of Mass, vespers, and *a cappella* motet for the most various liturgical occasions and purposes. This tradition is still to be found, unaltered, in the young Bruckner.[77]

The Romantic quarrel about "the true church music," which in practice had begun with the restorational tendencies of Johann Adam Hiller, C. P. E. Bach, and the rest, and had then been carried on in countless writings of Johann Friedrich Reichardt, J. A. P. Schulz, Herder, Kaspar Anton von Mastiaux, E. T. A. Hoffmann, A. F. J. Thibaut, and others, was non-denominational in nature and inextricably mingled with those restorational movements in both faiths that led to the revival of old music and to composing anew upon its model. The concept of "old masters" stems from the Romantic period. The countless motet collections of the time bear witness to the desire for "pious' and "edifying" church music. Numerous composers, beginning with Kaspar Ett and Johann Kaspar Aiblinger on the Catholic side, Johann Gottfried Schicht and Bernhard Klein on the Protestant, pursued this aim. Their most important later representative may have been Felix Mendelssohn, who, beyond denominational loyalty, was, paradoxically, perhaps the most churchly among the great German composers of the 19th century. In his extensive and many-sided creativity, church music may claim to outweigh the rest. Classicism triumphs in his concerted as in his *a cappella* works; they, too, can serve as indirect witnesses to the "Romantic" spirit, only insofar as they cannot be understood without the historicizing vein that ran through Romantic musical thinking. Close to Mendelssohn stand Eduard August Grell and Moritz Hauptmann, and with this group in turn the motet works of Johannes Brahms are closely linked. This trend was carried further on the Catholic side by Liszt, Josef Rheinberger, and Bruckner, then by the multitudinous composers of the Cecilian movement, and on the Protestant side by Heinrich von Herzogenberg (though himself a Catholic), Arnold Mendelssohn, Albert Becker, and many others, and finally by Max Reger (also a Catholic), though its tendency had long since turned away from

77. For a survey of the composers, cf. *ibid.*

the broad stream of Romantic composition and had become an internal concern of the church.

While all these efforts grew out of basic Classic and a-Romantic—often anti-Romantic—assumptions, Catholic church music in this period succeeded in creating a new and independent type of composition arising altogether from the Classic-Romantic spirit—namely, the symphonic Mass. Successor to the old concertante Mass, it is distinguished therefrom through its more strongly personalized expression, its more autonomous formal structure (not infrequently resting on the symphonic forms of sonata, rondo, etc.), through its more freely imaginative treatment of choruses and vocal solos, but above all through the independent and sometimes leading role of the orchestra, which from an accompanying and concertante body has now come to co-operate in building up form and expressiveness. Mozart's Requiem (however questionable the form in which it has been handed down to us), Haydn's six late Masses, and Beethoven's Mass in C, Op. 86, may have provided the initial basis; yet once again it was Beethoven who with his *Missa solemnis* set the pattern typical for the symphonic Mass throughout the whole 19th century. Whether the sole conceivable model from an earlier period, Bach's B minor Mass, played a role in this we need not discuss here. The masters of the 19th-century symphonic Mass linked up with Beethoven. Schubert's three Masses, in G (1815), A♭ (1822), and E♭ (1828), Berlioz's *Grande Messe des Morts* (1837), Liszt's *Gran Festival Mass* and Requiem, (both 1869), Bruckner's three grandiose late Masses, in D minor (1864), E minor (1866), and F minor (from 1867 on), and countless similar works cannot be imagined without Beethoven's example, and this sphere of influence further extends to Verdi's *Manzoni Requiem* (1874). Brahms's *Deutsches Requiem* (1857–68) stands between symphonic Mass and oratorio. To the degree that there is so much Romanticism in this branch of composition, there is no denying that the symphonic Mass—though in individual cases composed for liturgical purposes and taken up in divine service—can claim to be far more at home in the concert hall than in the church, that its treatment of the orchestra not infrequently comes close to opera, and that with it church-music composition in the stricter sense has indeed stepped out of its original frame.

Like the church music of both denominations, and in many ways closely related to it, the oratorio occupied an extensive field in 19th-century composition. Born of a spirit of revival and historicism similar to that of church music—though in its forms and treatment of sound material it leaned much more upon secular music and especially upon opera—the Romantic oratorio came to occupy a curious sort of intermediary position between church music, opera, and secular choral music. It developed no single uniform type, and between the markedly ecclesiastical and biblical oratorios like those of Bernhard Klein (1822–28) and the purely secular ones such as the two by Schumann, every intermediate stage is represented. Between 1819 and 1839 Friedrich Schneider cultivated the biblical oratorio in a style loosely leaning on Handel, and Mendelssohn did the same (1836 and 1846) in a manner similarly related to Bach. The much-performed *Zerstörung Jerusalems* (1829) of Karl Loewe seeks stronger dramatic expression and orchestral effects, and Liszt's *Die Legende von der Heiligen Elisabeth* (1867) and *Christus* (1873) in their approach and in their means already come close to Wagner's *Parsifal*. Research is still a long way from having dealt adequately with the place of the oratorio in the history of Romantic music. We cannot attempt here to give any even partially satisfactory presentation of the relationship of this form to the other forms of Romantic music, just as we must forego any proper survey of Romantic choral music, characteristic though it is in its witness to the specifically Romantic feeling for music revealed in its various types for men's, women's, and mixed chorus as well as to the historical continuity from Schubert to Janáček.[78]

It may be considered a recognized historical fact that in the 19th century German instrumental music of all categories was dominant in Europe, that composers of other countries took heed

78. Cf. in MGG, article *Chor-Komposition,* particularly 1385 ff., *Frauenchor* and *Männerchor.*

of it and in many cases learned from it or even studied in Germany itself. On the other hand, it must also be regarded as an incontestable historical fact that German and Austrian church music (oratorio, choral music, etc.) remained with rare exceptions a specifically German species, standing for the most part outside international connections and taking root only in its native land. However, in the field of opera, national importance is quite differently distributed. In Germany the period begins under the mark of that longing for a serious German national opera [79] which had found perfect fulfillment only in the one happy instance of *The Magic Flute*. Here, despite the pure Classicism of its forms and language, the Romantic tendencies are palpable: the fairy-tale material, the national character of the melodies, the profusion of stage effects, and much else; and whatever its other sources, German romantic opera —Hoffmann's *Undine* (1813), Spohr's *Faust* (1813), Weber's *Der Freischütz* (1821)—is linked with *The Magic Flute*. The processes that led to this type of opera, the influences from opéra-comique, the heritage taken over thence from Georg Joseph Vogler's Mannheim-Darmstadt "Tonschule," etc., are not for us to discuss here, nor is the question of how many elements of opera buffa were included in it. With its motifs from nature, its forest enchantment, with its ghostly Wolf's-Glen music, with its adoption of popular national song and dance, with its struggle between divine and infernal powers, with its male-chorus and waltz effects, *Der Freischütz* set a German-Romantic stamp on a type of opera that passed on through Heinrich August Marschner and various minor figures, and is still recognizable in Wagner's *Der fliegende Holländer*.

Yet this type alone by no means ruled the German stage. Beside it stood the Italian buffa and semi-seria operas of composers like Saverio Mercadante, Donizetti, and Bellini, and after Rossini had begun his triumphal progress across the stages of Europe with his *L'Italiana in Algieri* (1813) and *Il Barbiere di Siviglia* (1816), Germany, too, fell victim to the Rossini craze, during which the operas of this late master of a long history of Italian opera buffa

79. Cf. *Classic Music*, p. 71.

were among the most frequently performed.

The grand opera of French origin found an important master in Spontini, who was active and well-known in Germany; [80] the operas of Étienne-Nicolas Méhul, Rodolphe Kreutzer, Charles-Simon Catel, and others were apparently less at home in that country. By way of Grétry and his successors, the French revolutionary and rescue opera worked its way into Germany (in terms of genre, Beethoven's *Fidelio* belongs here), to be followed later by Daniel-François-Esprit Auber with his *Muette de Portici* (1828), Rossini with his *Guillaume Tell* (1829), and others. In addition, the Italian opera buffa was a particularly favorite genre on the German stage; Cimarosa, Paisiello, Paër, and many more were continually being performed. With François-Adrien Boieldieu and Louis-Joseph-Ferdinand Hérold, further foreigners won the German public's favor. Thus, when Meyerbeer's grand operas—*Robert le Diable* (1831), *Les Huguenots* (1836), *Le Prophète* (1849)—and Jacques-François Halévy's spectacular success, *La Juive* (1835), reached Germany, the precedence of Italian and French opera, however basically a-Romantic they were, seemed assured in this homeland of Romanticism. Not by chance did the writers of Schumann's circle and the young Richard Wagner turn, embittered, against these very types of opera.

Germany's own contribution—Friedrich von Flotow's *Martha* (1847), Albert Lortzing's *Zar und Zimmermann* (1837), *Der Wildschütz* (1842), and *Undine* (1845), or Otto Nicolai's *Die lustigen Weiber von Windsor* (1849)—remained modest by international standards; this was at best a minor lyric art, the theatrical parallel to the other small lyric forms, honest and middle-class, though with a touch of fairy-tale quality, not a full-scale opera at all, and furthermore it could lay only very limited claim to being considered "Romantic" in the full sense of the word. From the Classic period, Gluck's operas still survived to a certain extent; Mozart's *Clemenza di Tito* and especially *Don Giovanni* were still

80. Cf. E. T. A. Hoffmann, *Nachträgliche Bemerkungen zu Spontinis Oper Olympia* (Supplementary Remarks on Spontini's Opera *Olympia*), 1821.

in the repertory, but these, too, gradually faded out in the new Romantic period. The great project of a German national opera, which would then have been a full-scale Romantic opera able to hold its own against Italian and French opera, did not prosper. The Romantic movement, however longingly it looked toward the operatic stage, found there no master who could have fulfilled its dreams.

Such a figure did not appear until Richard Wagner, whose *Der fliegende Holländer* (1843), *Tannhäuser* (1845), and *Lohengrin* (1850) were soon to lead up to the "art work of the future," the "Gesamtkunstwerk"—a work for the stage in which music and poetry stood on an equal footing with each other and with all the other arts, an embodiment of all the synesthetic strivings of the Romantic age. It found its perfect realization in the trilogy of *Der Ring des Nibelungen* (1853–74), *Tristan und Isolde* (performed in 1865), *Die Meistersinger von Nürnberg* (performed in 1868), and *Parsifal* (1882), and its esthetic foundation in countless writings, above all *Oper und Drama* (1851). Despite all the propaganda and polemics, Wagner's music-dramas did not manage to drive the operas of other composers, older or contemporary, from the stage; they were too exacting in content, in musical structure, in technique of performance, to succeed in this. Gounod, Thomas, Bizet, Delibes, Chabrier, Massenet, and others always remained at home on the German stages, as did Verdi, and later Mascagni, Leoncavallo, Puccini, Eugène d'Albert, and many others. But with Wagner an historic event took place: for the first and only time, the German Romantic spirit broke through onto the international scene. Increasingly, it took over the opera stages of other countries, France in particular, and "wagnérisme" became simply the collective concept for the late Romantic music of the "new Germany." From his own later years through the period of National-Socialistic ideology, Wagner, for good or ill, epitomized the essence of the German in music. While this represented a markedly one-sided emphasis, it nevertheless revealed a final outburst of Romantic musical thinking, and its historical influence was immeasurable. German opera, for the first time since Mozart, takes an au-

thoritative part in the international repertory with the work of
Wagner in its various aspects: his choice of subject matter; the
inexhaustible symphonic texture of his orchestral writing, which is
woven from the constant leitmotives and within which are embed-
ded the so-called "endless melody" and the more or less closed
forms of vocal solos, ensembles, and choruses; his superabundance
of emotion and his insatiate rhetoric; his dramatic pathos and his
lyric ecstacy; his propensity for the transcendental and the legend-
ary; the blunt yet serene everyday quality of *Die Meistersinger,*
and the mystic-religious sublimity of *Parsifal.*

His contemporaries sensed what was revolutionary and over-
powering in Wagner more keenly than what was tradition-bound
or merely intensified. No one else caused such division of opinion.
The quarrels between his unconditionally devoted followers (from
Carl Friedrich Glasenapp and Houston Stewart Chamberlain to
Bernard Shaw and Guy de Pourtalès) and his embittered oppo-
nents (from Hanslick to Stravinsky) ranged over every level, from
objective controversy to hate-inspired malice, for half a century
and more. They only demonstrate what an immense and elemental
force the late phase of German Romanticism projected into the or-
derly progress of music history. With Wagner it also became clear
how deeply divided in their view of music were tradition-saturated
Classicism and the revolutionary "music of the future."

In practice, composers took a position between the two extremes. Of the "circumpolars" (as the eminent German musicolo-
gists Theodor Kroyer called them) like Siegfried Wagner, August
Bungert, Cyrill Kistler, Friedrich Klose, Engelbert Humperdinck,
and many others, who sought to carry on and even to outdo Wagner's style of opera, not one could approach him in intensity of effect or quality of composition. Indeed, only at the very end of the
Romantic era did a musician of equal rank make his appearance;
Richard Strauss—with *Salome* (1905), *Elektra* (1909), *Der Rosenkavalier* (1911), *Ariadne auf Naxos* (1912), etc.—could
match Wagner in dramatic-musical talent and, within the much-
altered context of a realistic, naturalistic, and veristic period of
opera, put forth new ideas based on the Wagnerian model, thus

bringing to German opera renewed world successes. The extent to which Strauss is to be regarded as still "Romantic" is open to question.

In opera, as in all areas of vocal music, the image of the Romantic period lingers on illumined by an opalescent twilight. To what extent the basic music-esthetic ideas of Romanticism (before and aside from Wagner) were carried out in operatic composition; to what esthetic, social, literary, and other backgrounds the operatic jumble of the 19th century may be traced; in what measure and in what way the great opera composers of the 19th century in the various countries influenced each other; who took here and who gave there (think of the still endlessly discussed Wagner-Verdi relationship); whether a relatively unified guiding idea of music-drama underlay the whole, as had unequivocally still been the case in the Classic period, or whether in fact only the arbitrary forces of uncontrolled and subjectively exaggerated individualism kept the ball rolling—these and many similar questions have never yet been clarified. One thing is sure, however: because of opera (and related genres such as ballet, operetta, etc.) the "supremacy of instrumental music," which had served as a fundamental principle for the 19th century, underwent a considerable retrenchment. In the public musical activity of both composer and consumer, opera took a conspicuous place beside instrumental music; even though the overwhelming majority of the operas produced in the 19th century have been forgotten, the lists of composers' works prove how extensively and intensively opera, as the second great form of music composition alongside the symphony, was grappled with. These lists show, furthermore, that alongside the ideas of the Romantic era—and underlying them—other ideas were current, of national, esthetic, literary, social, or whatever provenance, which went on developing independently. They make it clear that German Romanticism was only *one* facet in the music history of the 19th century, and no area proves this so strikingly as that of opera.

Things are much simpler in the realm of the song because here Schulz, Reichardt, Zelter, André, Zumsteeg, *et al.* (to say nothing

of Haydn, Mozart, and Beethoven) had already developed a distinct type in the Classic period, which then remained basic in the
German-speaking countries. Schubert did not interfere with it, only
developed it further. The lied (in its most important form, the solo
song with piano accompaniment) became "in its close linking of
poetry and music, of content and form, of voice and accompaniment, something so specifically German that the German lied and
song in general were regarded as identical"; [81] indeed, because of
this historical situation, this German word was taken directly into
the French and English languages, on occasion even into Italian.
What happened was at first nothing other than what Johann Christian Lobe had explained to Goethe in a simple and convincing
manner in 1820: the vocal part retained its "folk" flavor (though
this had grown more flexible and sensitive) and only the piano
part became richer, achieved greater independence and power of
characterization, while strophic variation allowed the composer to
adapt himself to changing content. To this extent the songs of
Schubert's early and middle period are thoroughly Classical songs.

That this groundwork was affected by such influences as the
Zumsteeg-Bürger type of ballad, the Italian type of operatic scena,
the French romance, and others, altered only the technical means,
not the nature of the lied. It became "Romantic" in the stricter
sense only when specifically Romantic poetry (Schubert's settings
of Schlegel, Novalis, Wilhelm Müller, and the rest) intensified the
emotional content of the composition, and when composers began
to divide their attention between the emotionally motivated but
still "songlike" leadership of the voice and the independently descriptive piano accompaniment that provided the quasi-symphonic
underpainting and eventually carried out its own imaginative developments beyond the specifications of the text (especially beginning
with Schubert's latter settings of the *Wilhelm Meister* songs and his
Schöne Müllerin). Herewith the strictly "Classic" ideal of the song
was shattered and a type of song composition achieved that re-
pressed the text in favor of the descriptive power of the music. Between a more Classical position, slowly becoming anemic and

81. Kurt Gudewill in MGG, article *Lied,* 766.

classisistic (Ludwig Berger, Bernhard Klein, Friedrich Heinrich Himmel, Friedrich Wilhelm Kücken, Mendelssohn, Peter Joseph von Lindpaintner, and countless later composers), and a more characterizing and programmatic tendency (Norbert Bürgmuller, Schumann, Robert Franz, Adolf Jensen; an intermediate position was taken by, for example, the Austrian Johann Vesque von Püttlingen), the German solo song continued its evolution throughout the 19th century in a variety of forms, mixtures, and compromises. The last great master who attempted once more to rebuild it anew from its original foundations was Johannes Brahms.

The ballad was cultivated as a specifically Romantic sub-category from Karl Loewe to Bruch, Humperdinck, Richard Strauss, and others. Not until Wagner, Liszt, and particularly Hugo Wolf, did the lied arrive at a crisis in which the very foundations of the genre were shaken through its convergence with the Wagnerian operatic style. The late Romantic masters of the German song like Richard Strauss, Gustav Mahler, Hans Pfitzner, and others were unable to restore the genre's former unity. But in its basic forms and its finest examples as well as in the "poetic idea" it continually endeavored to embody, the German lied of the 19th century (which also stimulated countless composers in France, England, Italy, Russia, Czechoslovakia, the Scandinavian countries, and so forth), was one of the most distinctive manifestations of Romantic musical thinking, with all its unsatiated yearnings, its deep feeling for nature, its warmheartedness and not infrequent sentimentality, and its proximity to national or folk music.

Along with piano and chamber music, the lied in the 19th century provided the strongest support of music in the home. The amateur singer took his place beside the amateur fiddler and the amateur pianist; like trio and quartet playing or piano four-hands, at least among the German middle-class, the singing of songs and duets remained well into the 20th century one of the basic, one of the most solid ways of fostering music. These were the types of composition that closely linked the broad circles of amateur performers with art music, keeping their love of music awake more vigorously than did symphony or opera, which were accessible to comparatively more restricted groups. Nothing so sharply divides the "new music" from the last echoes of Romanticism as the end of this practice of home music-making, so closely allied with the song, chamber music, and piano music of the period. The end of this association presaged the threatening division between amateurism and professionalism, between music of the past and music of the present.

V

The End of the
Romantic Era in Music

In the over-all context of music history, the Romantic era can only be understood as a partial phenomenon within the unity of a Classic-Romantic period. Its genres and forms, the foundations of its style, and even in many cases the composers themselves, it shares in common with the Classic era. Beethoven is a Romantic Classic or a Classical Romantic, and many a later composer is "more Classic" than he. The lofty ideas brought forth by Romanticism were rooted in Herder, Fichte, and later even in Goethe; the special qualities of musical forms and style brought forth are intensifications and developments, variants or limitations, in the last analysis perhaps also excrescences and extravagances—all of which, however, grew out of continuing elaboration of the High Classic style and its forms. There is no Romantic composer who does not stand fast upon the Classic canon of elements and forms, just as there is no Classic composer in whom there do not appear the beginnings of Romantic enrichment of form and intensified expression. From the pre- and early Classical figures around Jommelli, Rousseau, and Stamitz on to Richard Strauss, Reger, and Pfitzner, there extended a complete, unbroken period of music history although through deep internal contradictions, national antagonisms, and the tension between idealistic conservatism and realistic-naturalistic liberalism, its unity is indeed stretched to its limits, overstrained, and finally torn apart.

To mark the beginning of this period of music history, one could easily set the names of an Italian, a Frenchman, and a German side by side, as we have just done: one could multiply them by any number of names chosen from the three nations. To mark the end of what may with some justification be called the musical "Romantic Era," one is obliged willy-nilly to set down three German names. For although the Tchaikovskys and Mussorgskys, the Smetanas and Dvořáks, the Faurés and Debussys, the Respighis and Malipieros, the Elgars and Vaughan Williamses were still bound by many ties to German Romanticism, in one area or another of their being they remain outside the specifically Romantic circle. An excellent example of this is Verdi, who all his life took care not to let himself be placed in any artistic relationship with Wagner, and probably correctly. For Verdi's work is the characteristic product of a special development that by and large ran its independent course via Donizetti, Bellini, and lesser masters, on Italian soil (although under many influences from opéra-comique, grand opera, German romantic opera, etc.); after him this development continued (once again under the most varied influences, from French literature, Bizet, Wagner, Strauss, and Leoncavallo) ultimately to reach the naturalism and *verismo* of Puccini.

This picture, albeit drastically simplified, makes it clear that there were in the 19th century paths of development running alongside "Romanticism" in the narrower sense, influenced by it at times but on the whole led rather by autochthonous national forces and therefore not to be categorized outright as "Romantic" unless one is willing to degrade that concept to a mere synonym for "19th-century history." In general, presentations of music history light-heartedly subsume under the concept "Romantic" far too many things that have little or nothing to do with it. This is the reason, too, why in the main only the history of German music in the 19th century—with, of course, many side glances at other countries—allows itself to be classified under the "Romantic" rubric (and, even so, only in part), while Italian, French, and other music, despite all the influences from Germany, nevertheless remain preponderantly outside the Romantic domain.

A development similar to the Italian one took place in France, where a particular nationally conditioned trend began with Gossec

and Grétry. True, this was strongly influenced in its theories by
E. T. A. Hoffmann, in its practice by Beethoven, Schubert, and
Weber; [82] true, Cherubini and, later, Rossini made an impression
here, too, and Berlioz cast his lot mainly with the German neo-Romantics; but the course of history that leads from the revolutionary
opera to the grand operas of Spontini, Meyerbeer, and Halévy,
that expresses itself in the spirit of Liszt's and Chopin's piano
works and exerted its widest influence in the brilliance of the German pianists in Paris, and in the wittily sarcastic social criticism
that Offenbach dispensed in a manner more French than any
Frenchman's—this course after all went its way independently
alongside German Romanticism. Only when the influence of Wagner made itself felt (from the 1860s on) did German Romanticism
temporarily predominate over French individuality. Frenchmen
from Vincent d'Indy and Emmanuel Chabrier to Romain Rolland
and even Debussy made the pilgrimage to Bayreuth. Wagner's
works took hold in Paris, and the French Wagner party, supported
by Baudelaire, Verlaine, and Mallarmé,[83] was hardly less enthusiastic, devoted, and fanatical than the German. Henri Duparc,
D'Indy, and Chabrier form a sort of French "circumpolar" group.
But, despite all this, French music stood firm on its own national
"Classic" footing—that is, on the boundary line between late Baroque, Rococo, and earliest Classic period that bears the names of
Rameau and Couperin—and at intervals again and again redi-
rected itself according to that tradition. Thus, however often the
two streams temporarily flowed into each other, in the end French
music ran its course parallel to German Romanticism, and the
"French Romanticism" of Berlioz and César Franck is at bottom
as far removed from the German Romanticism of Weber and Wagner as is the "French neo-Classicism" of Gounod and Saint-Saëns
from the German variety of Mendelssohn and Brahms. By the
same token, figures like Bizet and Charpentier are not entirely
comparable with Otto Nicolai and Peter Cornelius, or with Verdi
and Mascagni.

82. Cf. MGG, article *Frankreich,* 781 ff.
83. *Ibid.,* 784.

In Spanish and Czech music of the 19th century things similarly followed their own special courses; we need not go into them in the present analysis. We are concerned here with an historical problem unique to the Romantic period. In earlier epochs of music history—the Renaissance, for example—the different nations all begin at the same level; then in the course of events one or another takes the upper hand and develops some sort of prototype that the others recognize (though they move away from it along their own lines) and in which they are all at one when it comes to composition in the main international genres. However, in the era of Romanticism the individual European nations are rooted in deeper historical foundations, from which they draw strength enabling them to follow up their own lines of development alongside the central manifestation. These lines often touch, absorbing influences from each other, but in the main they remain nationally determined and apply this nationally determined style to all genres and forms, even those that are standard for all Europe (as in this case, say, symphony or opera). Herein lies a fundamental difference between the Classic-Romantic period and all earlier periods of music history.

In the 19th century this new and distinctive basic situation is paralleled and often intersected by a second process (although it has not as yet been perceived how these procedures and basic elements related in detail to each other within the individual nations): namely, the development of a kind of neo-nationalism (sometimes also called "national Romanticism"—quite imprecisely, out of a superficial understanding of the concept of Romanticism). One of the most decisive and most admirable achievements of the High Classic period had consisted in the coming together of the styles of the separate nations, following a period of "mixed taste," into what Gluck and Chabanon called the "universal language," an "art of humanity" (Herder), a language in which differences in rank and station, country and religion had been resolved into a creed of humanity and world citizenship. This was the language of Haydn and Mozart, in which Beethoven participated too (with reservations here, divergences there). But one should not overlook the fact that this universal language (from whatever elements it may have coalesced) was German, German with a Viennese accent, and that alongside this universal language the national tongues continued to be spoken.

Romanticism, with its emphasis on national differences, contradictions, evaluations, broke into this world of cosmopolitan and humanitarian ideals. German Romanticism was so emphatically and penetratingly German that it lost this cosmopolitan character and in other countries was no longer considered as the result of an integration, but as a German claim to hegemony, in which (to continue the metaphor) the North German, and (with Wagner) the Saxon accent, pressed to the fore more vigorously than a universal language could bear. While Wagner, faced with the question "What is German?," found himself, as he confessed, "in ever greater confusion," Schumann perpetrated sentences that were just plainly offensive to other nations, such as "The highest peaks of Italian art do not even reach to the first beginnings of truly German art," or "The elevation of the German sensibility through German art may even today be regarded as the goal of our efforts." These assumptions led to that neo-nationalism in which the European nations split off from the universal stem and developed national idioms that cannot properly be called "languages" because, though springing from the original Classic-Romantic canon of elements and forms that was being upheld in Germany too, they nevertheless differ perceptibly, consciously, and often emphatically from the German musical tongue: they are, in other words, a sort of national dialect of the universal language. Their grammar and syntax continue (with reservations) to be that of the Classic-Romantic canon, but their expression and speech melody are national, regional, often conditioned by folklore.

This is the historical process that explains the splitting off of national musics from the main trunk of Classic-Romantic German music—to which they nevertheless remain attached as even the outermost branch does to its tree: Russian music from Glinka via Dargomizhsky, Tchaikovsky, Rimsky-Korsakov, Balakirev, Borodin, Cui, Mussorgsky, up to one of the last true late Romantics of

Russian music, the young Stravinsky; Czech music from Tomášek and Voříšek via Smetana and Dvořák to the Czech counterpart of Richard Strauss and Debussy, Janáček; Scandinavian music from Gade and Halfdan Kjerulf via Grieg, Rikard Nordraak, Andreas Hallén, August Söderman, Wilhelm Petersen-Berger, to Finn Höffding, Kurt Atterberg, and Gösta Nystroem; Hungarian music from Franz Erkel, Mihály Mosonyi, Emil Ábrányi, and Liszt to Bartók and Kodály; and the rest. However much their dialects, the tones of their speech or whatever one calls them, may diverge from the German, in elements and forms they all sprang thence and in the last analysis the language group was never altogether broken up.

Against this background also belongs the "English Renaissance"—the resurrection, after the decline during the late 18th and early 19th centuries, of a national English school (W. Sterndale Bennett, Henry Hugh Pierson, Sir Hubert Parry, Charles Villiers Stanford, and others), which sprang directly out of the German Romantic school. The renaissance later liberated itself and achieved an English idiom more or less its own (Sir Alexander Mackenzie, Sir Frederic Cowen, Sir Edward Elgar, and the Gilbert and Sullivan operettas), which ultimately arrived at an "English late Romanticism," in the specifically English musical language of a Vaughan Williams and a Benjamin Britten.

It is difficult to judge whether one should see a similar process for France in the continuity that led from César Franck, Lalo, Saint-Saëns, d'Indy, Chausson, Chabrier, and Dukas to Fauré, Debussy, and Ravel, because the French idiom in music had been inherited, as the German had been, from its own national past and did not have to be newly created. Yet French Impressionism in many respects forms a counterpart to the other national schools of the late 19th and early 20th centuries, and this the more so since, despite all its influence upon composers of other countries, it remained predominantly a French affair. Hence one may see in it the specifically French form of a national late Romanticism.

The universal and humanitarian age of Classicism was at the same time the great revolutionary age and the age of dawning nationalism, the age of the breaking down of class distinctions. With it began the decay of the supranational culture that since the Middle Ages had held the upper ranks of European society together despite all national hostilities. The musical reflection of this situation in the history of culture is the unique upsurge of a universal language embracing all mankind, round about which, however, the national tongues remained alive, and which itself forthwith broke up into any number of European dialects.

Here we have the most complicated problem of nationality that has ever appeared in any age of music history; indeed, the Romantic era is really the first period in that history when national distinctions exercised a decisive influence on the course of artistic development and were themselves cultivated into carefully nurtured chauvinisms. The consequence was a Babylonian confusion of tongues such as no previous period in music history had known. For in all previous periods the special idioms either remained an internal matter for the respective nations—the German polyphonic lied, for example, in the 15th and 16th centuries, English consort music in the 17th—or they became in turn international models, like Lully's instrumental compositions or Corelli's chamber sonatas. In the 19th century, however, while these national products came to be relished by an international public, none of them managed to achieve the position of an international model. Wagner's music-drama still came nearest to this goal. But it, too, went under in the general disintegration of the nations. A practical result of this process was that while outstanding achievements by individual composers could be assured a permanent place in the international repertoire, the great mass of composers and their works—and in no other period of music history was such an incredible amount of composing going on—found recognition in only the smallest circles and on the international scene remained entirely unknown. Compare with this the situation in earlier periods—especially in the Renaissance, when it was taken for granted that considerable quantities of Netherlandish, French, Italian, Spanish, English, and German music should achieve their place in the international market, exercising a mutually fructifying influence upon each other—

and there emerges the vivid paradox that the end of the Romantic era was indeed a time of excessive international activity for a "world class" of composers and practical musicians, but for the broad majority a time of sad provincialism.

In connection with retrospective interest in national pasts, with the enormous quantitative increase in musical composition, and with Romanticism's leaning toward antiquity, a further special problem arises that no other earlier period knew to even remotely the same extent: namely, that of *historicism* and of the schism between conservative inertia and radical belief in progress that had not ceased to exist even by mid-20th century. Although since the break between *prima* and *seconda pratica* around 1600 a conservative undercurrent may have accompanied music history throughout more than three centuries (in the form of Palestrina and Lasso renaissances, of "true church music," restorationism and Cecilianism), and although benevolent ceremonies and representations may have assisted the ephemeral survival of many categories of music, like the medieval isorhythmic motets in the 15th century, opera seria in the late 18th, the Lully cult in France even into the 19th, never before had the broad mass of consumers of music been so clearly divided into a majority of those who honor the past and a minority of believers in progress as was the case in the 19th century, particularly after the appearance of Berlioz, Liszt, and Wagner.

The aggressive spirit of the *Neue Zeitschrift für Musik* and its circle attacked not only superficiality and indolence but also the always dangerous development of a party that sought to combat the new as such and to annihilate it in iconoclasm. This attitude becomes apparent early on, in Zelter's pronouncement on Beethoven as in Goethe's on Philip Otto Runge; from the battle over Wagner in Germany and France to the embittered feuds of the present over Expressionistic, twelve-tone, and serial music, it has ceaselessly led to the battlefield. From about the middle of the 19th century to the middle of the 20th, every composer of any sort of "modern" tendency has had to stand his ground against hot-tempered enmities and polemic writings on music, the stream of which swelled to

a veritable torrent in this round hundred of years. Brahms and
Wagner, Hugo Wolf and Richard Strauss—in contrast to composers of lesser rank stigmatized as "epigones"—did manage to be
more or less readily taken into the international repertory during
their lifetimes, if by this we mean that outside the professional
field, too, they achieved the recognition and respect of a wide
public as well as countless performances of their works.

Since the close of the Romantic era, however, the isolation of
composers has increased alarmingly, on the one hand because the
conservatism of a world-wide music consumption posed insur-
mountable obstacles to such general recognition, on the other because the national schools with their own sometimes massive new
production had moved so far apart that they had simply lost sight
of each other. It is significant that Richard Strauss first learned to
know the scores of many contemporary French composers through
the intermediary of Romain Rolland, and Rolland himself remarked that "one must realize that although the great men can
be loved by all men, the intermediaries between the great men
are more particularly national. They escape the notice of
foreigners." [84] Thus it could come about that composers of sufficient quality to be leaders in their national schools and who could
have laid claim to world rank—Reger, for example, Janáček, Albert Roussel, and Ralph Vaughan Williams—remained by and
large limited in influence by national boundaries, while the great
public from New York to Moscow, from Stockholm to Naples
clung—and still clings—to a "Classic-Romantic" repertory extend-
ing not much further than from Bach or Haydn to Brahms or
Strauss, from Donizetti or Rossini to Verdi or Puccini. The "new
music" of the second decade of the 20th century came up against a
situation in which it was unable to overcome the confusion, disrup-
tion, and disintegration resulting from each nation's adherence to
its own historical tradition.

In the development that led to such a situation, historicism, the
tendency to revive the "old"—i.e. Baroque and Renaissance music—played a decisive part. Even without this, the Italians had to

84. *Fragments d'un journal,* entry for May 20, 1899.

a certain extent always held fast to Palestrina and Carissimi, the French to Couperin and Rameau, the Germans to Graun and Handel, the English (with their "concerts of ancient music") to the masters of Tudor or Elizabethan times, but now the movement in all countries for the restoration of church music, led off by German Romanticism, brought in addition the revival of unknown "old masters." [85] This meant that a vigorous stream of ancient *a cappella* technique and counterpoint, long-bygone practices such as fugue, canon, and the cantus-firmus technique, penetrated the Classic-Romantic era, reinforced by the beginnings of musicological research [86] and a revival of contrapuntal study, which had accommodated itself to the Procrustean bed of "Palestrina counterpoint," with the remarkable consequence that right up to the present day, the composer is obliged to prove his mastery in three- or four-hundred-year-old skills. Countless composers of the Classic period—like Mozart himself—went through the school of Padre Martini, whose *Esemplare ossia saggio fondamentale pratico di contrappunto* (1774–75) had risen to the rank of a standard textbook. Cherubini's *Cours de contrepoint et de fugue* (c. 1820), Johann Georg Albrechtsberger's numerous writings on thorough-bass and on strict composition, and many others up to Heinrich Bellermann base their instruction exclusively upon a distant past, with no intention whatever of teaching contemporary forms and techniques—whereas Berlioz on the other hand, in his *Grand traité d'instrumentation et d'orchestration* (1844; revised by Richard Strauss in 1905) produced the basic textbook for handling the Romantic orchestra.

The Viennese Classicists themselves had opened the door to historicism by taking up the fugue again after Haydn's Op. 20 string quartets (1772). Mozart arranged Bach fugues and in *The Magic Flute* paid his tribute to the Romantic longing for a chivalric past with the scene of the men in armor, set in a Bachian style. Beethoven studied Bach's works (so far as they were known then) and paid homage to the fugue in a great many of his own composi-

85. Cf. pp. 114 f. and 160–161.
86. Cf. p. 121 f.

tions. How broadly and how deeply the Bach revival penetrated
musical creation, musical education, the formation of musical taste
in the 19th century, is still impossible to estimate. The more the
interest in music of past times grew, the more new editions of such
music were published, the more it was played and performed, the
more fresh stimuli did it receive from all directions—from the Italian Baroque, from the Netherlands masters of the Renaissance,
from the German 16th-century lied—so that the already plentiful
conservative tendencies were supplemented and confirmed by this
retrospective inclination. These tendencies led to the extensive revival of old music, to the copying and parodying of styles (as in
Reger and Feruccio Busoni, in Strauss and Ravel). In Germany
around 1900 they gave rise to a movement that reacted from wea-
riness with "Romanticism" by attempting a total renewal of
music in the spirit of the 16th and 17th centuries, in the process
failing to see how firmly this very effort was rooted in Romanticism. And above all, these tendencies permeated the new creativity
of the time. From Beethoven to Reger and Bruckner, there is not a
single composer who was not somehow influenced by historicizing
tendencies. Without Bach and Handel, Brahms would not have become Brahms; without Palestrina and Paisiello, Verdi would not
have become Verdi.

Thus conservatism and historicism finally led, at the close of
the Romantic period, to a state of affairs such as the history of
music had never yet seen: public and private musical activity, education, theory, esthetics were all subsisting on the more or less distant past. The cycle of reproduction, instruction, and creation had
come to a standstill. The connection between contemporary music
and the wide circles of music lovers of all nations, which around
1800 had still been very close and spontaneous, had vanished; the
understanding of contemporary music had shrunk more and more
to the small circles of the musically "cultured" or of professional
colleagues; "*l'art pour l'art*," with Debussy, Busoni, and others of
the same ilk, had to a considerable extent turned into the slogan of
snobbish irresponsibility, so that Rilke's "ivory tower" had almost
become the norm. Composers chose their paths; the musical audi-

ence chose a different one.

Nationalism, historicism, and the cleavage between inertia and progress are problems that had already appeared early in the Classic-Romantic period, but they came more strongly to the fore only with the advance of the Romantic concept of music and of Romantic composition. The same holds true of another special problem of Romanticism, namely, the priority of instrumental music, and, closely allied with this, the controversy over absolute music and program music. Not the Classic period, but rather the Classic-Romantic period was "the age of instrumental music" [87] and it started at the very point where most of the specifically Romantic features and problems of music began: with Beethoven. While the life-work of all previous masters is fairly evenly distributed between vocal and instrumental production (depending on demand and opportunity), and none of them—not even Haydn—shows a discernible preference for either one or the other, with Beethoven things changed. Not that he expressly proclaimed the priority of instrumental music (theorizing was not in his line)—but the importance of his sonatas, quartets, and symphonies made such a powerful impression on his contemporaries and left his vocal works so far behind in number and quality that the instrumental music automatically took precedence. In addition, it quite particularly kindled the enthusiasm of the Romantic writers; the historical significance of Hoffmann's review of the Fifth Symphony and his essay *Beethovens Instrumentalmusik* lies not so much in their recognition of an individual artist as in the fact that Beethoven's instrumental compositions obviously opened up to Hoffmann himself (and concomitantly to his contemporaries) the "language of the Infinite" and its content of "poetic ideas." Now suddenly vocal music appeared as a Pegasus yoked, the necessity of submitting to words and their interpretation a humiliating fetter. The composer had only to harken to his genius, to the voice of the Infinite, and make himself its priest; only in this way could music become the true "spirit-world of Djinnistan," "the only genuine Romantic art." Only the language of instruments could enable music to rise to its

87. Cf. *Classic Music*, p. 67.

highest task, to become the herald of eternal ideas.

This doctrine outlasted the Romantic period without, be it said, significantly diminishing the composition of vocal music in practice. Opera composers from Weber to Strauss did not regard their art as second-rate, any more than did song composers from Schubert to Pfitzner or male-chorus composers from Friedrich Silcher to August von Othegraven. But in the general view fostered by philosophers like Kant, Nietzsche, Schopenhauer, Eduard von Hartmann, Friedrich Hand, by writers on music like Hanslick, Ambros, Busoni, and others, the idea nevertheless took hold that "true music" lay in "pure," in "absolute" instrumental music, beside which the vocal categories were left to bear the odium of being considered music for the less demanding, for the broad mass of music lovers; and countless dilettantes as well as musicians adhered to such an evaluation till well into the 20th century.

This brought a further dichotomy to the already ambiguous situation of Romantic music, and the more so since at the beginning of the period the justification of instrumental music, or at least its ability to autonomously convey meaning, was still very much in doubt. Goethe still had a hard time understanding it, and Jean Paul felt far more sympathetic toward vocal than toward instrumental music. In Salomon Sulzer's *Theorie der schönen Künste* (1771 ff.), instrumental music is said to be "a lively and not unpleasant noise," Kant in his *Critique of Judgment* (1790) reproached it for "representing nothing," "a concept without a real referent," and even as late as 1783 (in an essay in Wieland's *Teutsche Merkur*) Ernst Wilhelm Wolf [88] expressly gives preference to vocal music. The idea of the unity of vocal and instrumental music and of their equality remained in the back of Hoffmann's mind, even though he leaned more and more toward the instrumental side.[89] In the eyes of nonmusicians, instrumental music only slowly acquired the status of a respectable art and only gradually freed itself of the clinging aftertaste of "applied" art, art for entertainment. Ludwig Tieck drew a comparison in his *Musikal-*

88. According to Schering, *Kritik des romantischen* . . .
89. *Ibid.*, pp. 94 and 282.

ische Leiden und Freuden between vocal and instrumental music that probably renders the attitude of the period around 1820 very well. He says, among other things, that vocal music "always seems to me . . . to be only a qualified art; it is, and will remain, intensified declamation and discourse. But in instrumental music art is independent and free, it prescribes its own laws, it improvises playfully and without set purpose, and yet attains and fulfills the highest; it simply follows its own dark impulse and in its dallyings expresses what is deepest and most wonderful. . . . These symphonies unveil in enigmatic language what is most enigmatic, they depend on no law of actuality . . . they remain in their purely poetic world. . . . The purpose itself is always immanent, and begins and ends the work of art."

Ideas like this remained fundamental to the understanding of instrumental music in the 19th century, but they were vigorously contested up to the days of Busoni and Pfitzner. Behind them lies the question concerning the fulfillment of meaning. Does "absolute" music express something? Does it in every case express something, or can it be a pure play of forms (which Hanslick never said, though it is often attributed to him)? What can it express? To what extent can it express clearly what is intended? How far can it get beyond vague and uncertain expression of feeling; to what degree can it make precise statements? Is it allowed to be symbolic only in the classic sense,[90] or may it use its tone-painting media to relate, to depict, to illustrate? Should Herder's "no shadow of anything perceptible" [91] still rule or should instrumental music assume the task of becoming naturalistic? Questions of this sort fired the literary polemics [92] on "absolute" and "program" music, which continued to flourish till the end of the Romantic period and still echo in the writings of Krenek and Stravinsky.

"The phantom dualism between 'applied' and 'absolute' music entered the European consciousness . . . boding ill and leading to serious conflicts." [93] If it were true that instrumental music could

90. Cf. *Classic Music,* p. 13.
91. *Ibid.*
92. Cf. MGG, articles *Absolut* and *Programm.*
93. Schering, *Kritik* . . . , p. 90 in *Vom musikalischen Kunstwerk.*

express only vague content or that it consisted only in a play of
beautiful forms, nothing justified its laying a claim to precedence;
but if it could be "the clear expression of special, characteristically
individual feelings" and the bearer of "a quite definite, clearly understandable individual content," it ran the risk of becoming the
object of guessing games and in certain circumstances must become the victim of "incomprehensibility." [94] "The inexhaustible
possibilities of music have now been opened up for us through
Beethoven's tremendous mistake." It was Beethoven—in his im-
petuous desire to render such "clearly understandable content" in
the language of pure instrumental music, which by its nature was
in any case capable of rendering content "only in its universality"
and for which it was "in truth impossible" to express itself so dis-
tinctly and unequivocally—who fell victim to a total error.

That was Wagner's judgment, and it remained the dilemma for
instrumental music during the whole Romantic period: it cradled
itself in the illusion of being able to express beyond all misunderstanding what its language was allowed only to outline by allusion.
In consequence it was driven—in part by composers who tried to
make their ideas comprehensible, in part by interpreters and listeners who sought to extract a "clearly understandable content"—
ever deeper into programmatic explication, into so-called poetic
hermeneutics, or directly into program music. Composers themselves often hinted at hidden programs—even Beethoven did so
occasionally, Schumann frequently, as did Berlioz, and hundreds
of lesser masters up to Debussy, Mussorgsky, Ravel, Dvořák,
Janáček and many others—although they just as often guarded
resolutely against any idea that the composition had grown out of
the program. According to Schumann, who incidentally declared
that he had learned more counterpoint from Jean Paul than from
his music teacher, "music needs no program"; it is always "self-
sufficient and explicit" (to Moscheles, September 22, 1837 [95]).
"He [Rellstab] probably thinks I get hold of a screaming child and

94. Richard Wagner, *Oper und Drama*, I, Leipzig, 1852, Ch. 5 (*Gesammelte Schriften*, III, pp. 277–79). The whole chapter is basic for the
understanding of the question in the 19th century.)
95. Schumann, *Briefe: Neue Folge*, Leipzig, 1886, p. 149.

try to find the corresponding notes. It's the other way round" (to Dorn, September 5, 1839). And as Beethoven, in order to forestall any naturalistic interpretations of its programmatic superscriptions, remarked about his Sixth Symphony: "More expression of feeling than painting," so Schumann said of his First: "I did not want to paint, to depict anything" (to Spohr, November 23, 1842). Again and again composers parried all inclination to take their programmatic indications too literally and to expect of music a more precise faculty of expression than it possesses.[96] Interpreters sought to make works that were difficult of access to the public more toothsome by suggesting programs, as Wagner himself did with Beethoven's works [97] or Josef Schalk with Bruckner's Seventh Symphony or, say, in the way Hermann Kretschmar did later in his three volumes of concert guides.

But other composers without hesitation wrote music that was intended to relate or depict, as symphonic poems do from Berlioz and Liszt onward, music that does not shrink from naturalism of any sort, though here of course there arises once again the problem of how such freely descriptive and pictorial music should find its most convincing form. Quite rightly, Wagner said from the point of view of the Romantic: "Nothing is less absolute than music," [98] but he did not fail to add in the same context: "If there were no form, there would certainly be no works of art." The "new form" is, according to Wagner, "program music," and music can allow itself to accede to this challenge because it can never lose its autonomy, because "in no association that it enters into [can] it cease to be the highest, the most redemptive art." [99] Busoni said: [100] "In reality program music is just as onesided and as limited as that type of tonal tapestry glorified by Hanslick, the so-

96. See Janáček concerning his piano pieces *On Overgrown Paths* (1902–08), *et passim* in his *Feuilletons*, 1959, e.g. p. 139 f.; also Richard Strauss to Romain Rolland cited above, fn. 28.

97. *Gesammelte Schriften*, V, p. 169 ff.

98. *Über Liszts symphonische Dichtungen* (1857) in *Schriften*, V, p. 182 f.

99. *Ibid.*

100. In his *Entwurf einer neuen Ästhetik der Tonkunst*, Trieste, 1907, p. 13. (English translation by Theodore Baker, New York, 1911).

called 'absolute music.' " The Romantic era left the question in its natural state of irresolution, and the retrospective criticism of musicology can only verify the facts. Every subsequent programmatic interpretation of Romantic instrumental music overshoots its mark if it proceeds along the lines of Goethe's epigram: "If you can't explain it, attribute something to it" (*Legt ihrs nicht aus, so legt was unter*). But no subsequent interpretation of this music can miss its aim altogether, because the demand that a work of art should express "a poetic idea" is inherent in the basic concept of Romantic music, and the interpreter may proceed on the assumption that the composer would have had some basic idea of this sort in mind. This holds for the innumerable "poetic" interpretations brought forth by the literature of the 19th and 20th centuries; it also holds for, among others, Arnold Schering's much-discussed interpretations of Beethoven.

None of the earlier periods of music history began with such a clear and ambitious integration of early efforts at a universal cosmopolitan-European style, none sprang so fully and radiantly armed from the head of Zeus as the Classic-Romantic era, and yet none was so soon torn by contradictions and cleavages, by literary controversies and musical dichotomies, by tormenting doubts of its own adequacy and by the overweening idea that the composer was godlike. Everything seemed to go to pieces, shipwrecked against the extremes of too much freedom and too much restraint. Between a cult of genius that bordered on sacrilege and a disdain of epigones that knocked the ground from under all unassuming craftsmanship, between the worship of music as a substitute religion and its degradation to the point of prostitution, the field of the possible and realizable stretched far and wide. And this resulted in the endless inherent problems, whose inexhaustibility constitutes an essential characteristic of the Romantic age.

Beside the few "special" problems which have been dealt with up to this point, countless others arose that we cannot attempt to touch upon here. The "music industry" became internationalized to the highest degree, but the nations lived more and more apart. Private cultivation of music flourished—but always further removed from contemporary composition; public musical activity became (especially in Germany) more and more the business of states and cities, once Wilhelm von Humboldt had perceived that in the early period of industrialism it would be more than ever important to attract the broad masses to music. The gradually increasing attempts that had been made by the successors of Zelter, Nägeli, and Schultz at popular education in music bore witness to the best intentions but were artificially directed and in the end bore little fruit. Upon the misconception that to achieve this purpose the autonomy of artistic creation should be circumscribed and the fundamentals of musical composition adapted to the popular listening habits of an earlier generation, is founded the interference of totalitarian states with the freedom of the composer. The need to provide the lightest and most superficial entertainment for those classes of society that were not at heart familiar with or interested in music lay at the opposite pole from the tenacity with which the overwhelming majority of music lovers and professional musicians held fast to serious cultivation of the Classic-Romantic repertory and from the arrogant esoterics of those tight little groups for whom the salvation of music was to be found only in radical experimentation. If the first ended up in the devastating lowest-common-denominator wasteland of a tin-pan-alley, and the second stifled in the unproductive stereotype of inherited conventions, the third proclaimed the total overthrow of its heritage without becoming aware that its activity was nothing other than a secondary neo-Romanticism.

At the very time, then, when the decline of music as a universal art, valid and binding for all humanity, was in full swing among Europe's masses, a "new music" addressed itself quite specifically to the small circle of the professionals, assiduously ignoring the fact that by this move the primal current of all music, the living circuit linking production, reproduction, and reception, was being cut off. The willing company of dilettantes, not understanding it and having no relation to it, around 1900 mistook a *fin de siècle* cultivation of music as "Romanticism," rebelled, refused to follow it, and turned to the shores of a faraway past. A disastrous abyss yawned between composer and public. The high-priestly function that artists had arrogated to themselves in the early stages of Romanticism degenerated into a cult of stardom, and the late stages were torn by divisions, antinomies, and heresies of every sort.

In historical retrospect it is almost impossible to recognize any overlapping uniformity in this confusion. Practical music-making and music-teaching continued to follow well-trodden paths without developing any new ideas or forms. As early as Hoffmann's time, the artist had become either the idol of society or its fool; now he put on Bohemian airs or withered away in some official capacity in the music world. While newly written music, because of its intellectual and technical demands, vanished ever further over the horizon of both the average musician and the dilettante, the foundations of musical education for the laymen and for children, out of which understanding of contemporary creativity should have been growing ever afresh, collapsed altogether. While trade-union and copyright organizations assured musicians of protection and a position in society such as they had attained in earlier times only in exceptional cases, the music-making masses rejected their music or lost contact with it. The official "music industry" became a décor concealing a threatening emptiness. The Classic-Romantic period, characterized in its beginnings by the convincing unity of all its forces and all its achievements, dissolved in chaos.

Hence the question "When did the Romantic era end?" evades any definite answer. If as a rule it is always easier to determine the beginning than the end of a period in music history (see above, p. 128 ff.) this holds true to a special extent for the Classic-Romantic era. Setting the boundaries of a period presupposes recognition of the fundamental unity governing it. While such a basic unity, contradictions and divergences notwithstanding, may be more or less convincingly defined for the older periods of music history, in regard to the Romantic era this is very difficult. The period remained coherent only at its deepest underpinning, its canon of elements and forms. The centrality of major-minor tonality was never seriously put in question from Pergolesi and Stamitz up to Debussy and Janáček; it was Schoenberg, Webern, and Stravinsky who first attempted to break up the system as such. Until their time, Classic periodicity, rhythm, meter, however stretched and strained, remained the substructure of all musical forms; and even afterward, only by laborious efforts was the way opened to the discovery of other principles on which to organize time. With Strauss, Kodály, Scriabin, Classic melody and thematic techniques still glimmer through the cloaking of a consciously anti-Romantic texture. The plan of sonata, rondo, song-form, dance and march forms, but also the traditional types such as fugue and canon, persisted under the shimmering mirror-surface of novel or quite free attempts at form; indeed, partly revitalized, they achieved great prestige. In Schoenberg's *Buch der hängenden Gärten,* Hindemith's *Marienleben,* and Stravinsky's *Petrushka,* it is difficult for the historian of today still to recognize the levers intended to overturn the last remnant of Romanticism. Two-thirds of the way through this 20th century, music is being made in every country of the globe on pianos of diatonic-chromatic tuning, and even if composers have turned away from the monster orchestral apparatus of Mahler and Strauss and have shown preferences for chamber-music groupings, the violin, the oboe, and the horn still bear witness to the same sounds and instrumental color-effects as ever. It was far easier to declare war on the Romantic heritage than to break free of it.

The Classic-Romantic period gradually died away around 1910. It dissolved in separate national and individual directions, abandoning the basic concepts from which it had originally sprung. The universal art of humanity lost its cosmopolitanism in a confusion of national dialects, in the clamor of egotistical private idioms, without being thereby released from the profound dichotomies of its inherent problems or made obsolete by the overwhelming unity of a new artistic intent. By constantly pushing outward at the frontiers of experimentation for more than half a century, the "new music" movement has facilitated Romanticism's survival. Whether it has come to an end as a historical period, nobody can say.

BIBLIOGRAPHY

This is a highly selective list, with emphasis on works in English; preference is given to titles easily available in paperback editions, which are indicated by asterisks.

GENERAL WORKS

*Abrams, M. H., *The Mirror and the Lamp: Romantic Theory and the Critical Tradition*, New York, 1948.

*Antal, Frederick, *Classicism and Romanticism*, New York, 1966.

*Arzt, F. B., *From the Renaissance to Romanticism: 1300–1820*, Chicago, 1962.

Babbitt, Irving, *Rousseau and Romanticism*, New York, 1919.

*Barzun, Jacques, *Classic, Romantic and Modern*, rev. ed., New York, 1961.

*Bate, Walter J., *From Classic to Romantic*, New York, 1961.

Bolgar, R. R., *The Classical Heritage and its Beneficiaries*, Cambridge, Mass., 1969.

*Brody, Jules, ed., *French Classicism: A Critical Miscellany*, New York, 1966.

Draper, John W., *Eighteenth Century English Aesthetics: A Bibliography*, New York, 1967.

Frye, Northrop, ed., *Romanticism Reconsidered*, New York, 1965.

Gay, Peter, *The Enlightenment: An Interpretation*, New York, 1966. New York, 1962.

*Gleckner, Robert F. and Gerald E. Enscoe, *Romanticism: Points of View*, New York, 1962.

Goethe, Johann W. von, *Goethe's Letters to Zelter with Extracts from those of Zelter to Goethe*, transl. and ed. A. D. Coleridge, London, 1892.

Halsted, John, ed., *Romanticism: A Collection of Documents*, New York, 1969.

Hazard, Paul, *European Thought in the Eighteenth Century: From Montesquieu to Lessing*, transl. J. L. May, New Haven, 1954.

Lovejoy, Arthur O., *On the Discriminations of Romanticisms*, in his *Essays in the History of Ideas*, Baltimore, 1948.

*Lucas, John L., *Decline and Fall of the Romantic Ideal*, Cambridge, Mass., 1948.

Robertson, John G., *Studies in the Genesis of Romantic Theory in the 18th Century*, New York, 1923.

Saisselin, Remy G., *Taste in Eighteenth-Century France*, Syracuse, 1965.

Schiller, J. F., *On the Aesthetic Education of Man*, transl. and ed. Elizabeth M. Wilkinson and L. A. Willoughby, London. 1967.

Smith, Logan Pearsall, *Four Words: Romantic, Originality, Creative, Genius,* London, 1924.

Wallach, L., ed., *The Classical Tradition,* Ithaca, 1969.

*Walzel, Oskar, *German Romanticism,* New York, 1966.

Wasserman, Earl R., ed., *Aspects of the Eighteenth Century,* Baltimore, 1965.

WORKS ABOUT MUSIC

Abraham, Gerald, *A Hundred Years of Music,* Chicago, 1964.

——*Slavonic and Romantic Music,* New York, 1968.

Bach, C.P.E., *Essay on the True Art of Playing Keyboard Instruments,* transl. and ed. William J. Mitchell, New York, 1949.

Barzun, Jacques, *Berlioz and the Romantic Century,* 3rd ed., New York, 1969 (*2nd ed., abridged, as *Berlioz and his Century,* New York, 1966).

Blume, Friedrich, *Geschichte der evangelischen Kirchenmusik,* Kassel, 1965.

Brook, Barry S., *La Symphonie française dans la seconde moitié du XVIIIe siècle,* Paris, 1962.

Bücken, Ernst, *Die Musik des Rokokos und der Klassik,* Potsdam, 1929.

Burney, Dr. Charles, *An Eighteenth-Century Musical Tour in France and Italy,* ed. Percy Scholes, London, 1959.

——*An Eighteenth-Century Musical Tour in Central Europe and the Netherlands,* ed. Percy Scholes, London, 1959.

Coeuroy, A., *The Musical Theory of the German Romantic Writers,* in *The Musical Quarterly,* XIII (1927), 108–29.

Einstein, Alfred, *Music in the Romantic Era,* New York, 1947.

Grout, Donald J., *A History of Western Music,* New York, 1960.

*Hanslick, Eduard, *The Beautiful in Music,* transl. Gustav Cohen, New York, 1891.

Hoffmann, E. T. A., *Selected Writings,* transl. and ed. Leonard J. Kent and Elizabeth C. Knight, Chicago, 1970.

Kurth, E., *Die romantische Harmonik und ihre Krise in Wagners "Tristan,"* Berlin, 1920. Reprint: Hildesheim, 1968.

Lang, Paul Henry, *Music in Western Civilization,* New York, 1941.

*Longyear, Rey M., *Nineteenth-Century Romanticism in Music,* Englewood Cliffs, N.J., 1969.

——*Schiller and Music,* Chapel Hill, N.C., 1966.

Mellers, Wilfrid, *Romanticism and the 20th Century,* London, 1957.

Newman, William S., *The Sonata in the Classic Era,* Chapel Hill, N.C., 1963.

————*The Sonata Since Beethoven,* Chapel Hill, N.C., 1970.

Rolland, Romain, *Goethe's Interest in Music,* in *The Musical Quarterly,* XVII (1931), 157–94.

*Schumann, Robert, *On Music and Musicians,* ed. Paul Rosenfeld, New York, 1946.

Strunk, Oliver, *Source Readings in Music History,* New York, 1950 (also paperback edition, 5 vols., New York, 1965.).

Tischler, Hans, *Classicism, Romanticism and Music,* in *The Music Review,* XIV (1953) 108–205.

Ursprung, Otto, *Katholische Kirchenmusik,* Potsdam, 1931.

BIOGRAPHICAL WORKS

BACH

Geiringer, Karl, *The Bach Family: Seven Generations of Creative Genius,* London, 1954.

BEETHOVEN

Anderson, Emily, transl. and ed., *Letters of Beethoven,* rev. ed., New York, 1964.

*Thayer, Alexander W., *Life of Beethoven,* rev. and ed. Elliot Forbes, Princeton, 1964.

BERLIOZ

Berlioz, Hector, *Memoirs,* transl. and ed. David Cairns, New York, 1969.

BRAHMS

*Geiringer, Karl, *Brahms, His Life and Work,* New York, 1947.

COUPERIN

Mellers, Wilfrid, *François Couperin and the French Classical Tradition,* London, 1950.

GLUCK

*Einstein, Alfred, *Gluck,* New York, 1955.

Gluck, C. W., *The Collected Correspondence,* ed. H. Asow, transl. S. Thomason, London, 1962.

HAYDN

*Geiringer, Karl, *Haydn, A Creative Life in Music,* rev. ed., Los Angeles, 1968.

Haydn, Joseph, *Collected Correspondence and London Notebooks,* ed. H. C. Robbins Landon, New York, 1959.

Landon, H. C. Robbins, *The Symphonies of Joseph Haydn,* London, 1955; supplement, 1961.

LISZT

*Searle, Humphrey, *The Music of Liszt,* New York, 1966.

MOZART

Anderson, Emily, ed., *Letters of Mozart and His Family,* 2nd ed., ed. A. Hyatt King and Monica Carolan, New York, 1966.
*Dent, E. J., *Mozart's Operas: A Critical Study,* 2nd ed., New York, 1960.
Deutsch, Otto Erich, *Mozart, A Documentary Biography,* transl. Eric Blom, Peter Branscombe, and Jeremy Noble, Stanford, Cal., 1965.
*Lang, Paul Henry, ed., *The Creative World of Mozart,* New York, 1963.

SCHUBERT

Brown, Maurice J. E., *Schubert: A Biography with Critical Digressions,* New York, 1958.
Deutsch, Otto Erich, *Schubert: A Documentary Biography,* transl. Eric Blom, London, 1947.

SCHUMANN

Plantinga, Leon B., *Schumann as Critic,* New Haven, 1968.

VERDI

*Toye, Francis, *Giuseppe Verdi, His Life and Works,* New York, 1946.

WAGNER

*Wagner, Richard, *Wagner on Music and Drama: A Compendium of Richard Wagner's Prose Writings,* ed. Albert Goldman and Evert Sprinchorn, New York, 1968.
White, Chappell, *An Introduction to the Life and Works of Richard Wagner,* New York, 1967.

INDEX

CLASSIC AND ROMANTIC MUSIC

A Comprehensive Survey

Renaissance and Baroque Music: A Comprehensive Survey
Translated by M. D. Herter Norton